NI'IHAU SHELL LEIS

NI'IHAU SHELL LEIS

Linda Paik Moriarty
Photographs by Leland and Christopher Cook

A Kolowalu Book
University of Hawaii Press
Honolulu

© 1986 University of Hawaii Press
All Rights Reserved
Printed in Singapore

04 03 02 01   10 9 8 7

Library of Congress Catalog Card No. 86-50306
ISBN 0-8248-0998-X

University of Hawai'i Press books are printed
on acid-free paper and meet the guidelines for
permanence and durability of the Council on
Library Resources.

Designed by Jill Chen Loui

**This book is dedicated to
the lei makers of Niʻihau.**

CONTENTS

Preface   9

Acknowledgments   11

Introduction: Shells and Man   12

History of the Niʻihau Shell Lei   15

Types of Shells Used in Niʻihau Leis   35

Collecting the Shells   64

Making a Lei   69

Styles of Sewing Shell Leis   79

Selecting a Lei   96

Care and Storage of Niʻihau Shell Leis   98

Appendix A. Scientific Descriptions of Niʻihau Shells   101

Appendix B. Niʻihau Shell Leis in Museum Collections   103

Bibliography   104

PREFACE

I first became interested in Niʻihau shell leis in the early 1970s when they were becoming increasingly popular. At this time a growing number of women could be seen wearing them, and many articles on the subject appeared in the Honolulu newspapers. Like many other women, I too wanted to own one of these lovely leis, but before making a choice I began to pay close attention to the different types. I observed that, in addition to the little ivory-colored shells strung in the simple, traditional way, shells of many different colors and types were used, made into a variety of lei styles. The very subtle differences in shell color and how these color variations determined the price of the lei was particularly interesting. The more Niʻihau shell leis I saw the more fascinated I became with all aspects of this beautiful art form.

At this time, I was given several leis which my father and uncle had acquired on Niʻihau where they were stationed for short periods during World War II. As I compared these leis from the 1940s with those made more recently, I realized that there were marked differences in the styles and in the use of certain shells. Puzzled by the obvious changes in the art form over the years I decided to go to the source—the lei makers themselves. These women and their ancestors had been practicing this art for generations, and from them I learned many of the intricate details of the shell craft: how and where the shells are gathered, the methods of sewing them, the names of the types and colors of the shells, and the names of the styles of the leis.

I began looking for published information on Niʻihau shell leis, but found very little material. What I did locate was usually sketchy and offered only general comments on the beauty of the leis and their widespread popularity. I was amazed that no one had ever documented the history and the techniques of this unique Hawaiian art form. Other Hawaiian arts, such as some of the intricate *lauhala* and *makaloa* plaiting, have been lost forever because of similar neglect. I became concerned that a similar fate might befall the Niʻihau shell lei and I set out to gather and record all the information on the leis that I could find.

An intensive search of many written sources again yielded little information. Many of the early explorers had observed the Hawaiians wearing shell ornaments, but they were primarily interested in the more striking ornamentations, such as feather cloaks and tattoos. Nonetheless, archaeological studies have determined that the use of shells for ornaments was widespread, including those of the Niʻihau type. This led me to begin extensive correspondence with the museums in Hawaiʻi and throughout the world which I knew had significant Hawaiian collections. My research yielded valuable information concerning the acquisition of leis by early explorers and traders. I was pleased to locate these leis and to know that they had been preserved and appreciated for many years. Eventually, I had the great good fortune to meet and interview many of the Niʻihau women who actively practice the art of shell lei making, and it is their observations and knowledge that comprise the bulk of the text.

Where my informants were unable to provide the Hawaiian names for shells or styles of leis, because modern terms and scientific names are more commonly used today, I referred to the works of Pukui and Elbert *(Hawaiian Dictionary)*, McDonald *(Ka Lei)*, and Titcomb *(Native Use of Marine Invertebrates in Old Hawaii)*. To provide scientific data on the shells used, I relied on E. Alison Kay and her publication *Hawaiian Marine Shells.* An appendix to my text by Dr. Kay gives specific scientific information on the shells.

The beautiful photographs that accompany the text were taken by Leland Cook, a photographer with Tiffany & Co. of New York for more than twenty-five years. Cook, assisted by his son Christopher, brought to the project their experience and technical skills in so photographing small objects that none of their color and detail is lost. The results speak for themselves.

I hope that this book will not only provide a definitive text on Niʻihau shell leis, but will also develop in the reader a deeper appreciation and understanding of the skill and effort required to create this beautiful and unique Hawaiian art form.

ACKNOWLEDGMENTS

I am deeply grateful to the following individuals who generously shared their time and knowledge and helped make this book possible: Barlow Chu, Aletha Kaohi, Charlotte Duval, Sue Hamabata, Ilei Kelley, Gabriel I, Benjamin Paik, Beatrice Lovell, Danita Aiu, Annette Bixler, Alina Malaki Kanahele, Lei Pahulehua, Renee Ness, Maile Andrade, Regina Kawamoto, Frank Hewitt, Connie Irons, Mililani Trask, Reginald Gage, Herman von Holt, Gladys Brandt, Yuklin Aluli, Dondi Ho Costa, Lyn Martin, Frances Frazier, Henry Taeza, and Barbara Steenhof.

I wish especially to thank the following individuals and institutions who allowed me to photograph leis from their collections: Miriam Pahulehua, Sherlin Niau Beniamina, Juliet Rice Wichman, Ruth K. Seto, Sophie Cluff, Alice Paik, Ida Hayselden, Jean Ariyoshi, Barbara Nishek, Grove Farm Homestead Museum, Bishop Museum, and the British Museum.

Special thanks to E. Alison Kay for her help in identification and scientific interpretation of the Ni‘ihau shells. Thanks also to Alfons Korn for providing me with valuable historical information and to William Kikuchi of Kauai Community College for archaeological information.

I appreciate the kind assistance of Roger Rose, Dora Jacroux, and Dorothy Weight of Bishop Museum; Robert Schleck of Grove Farm Homestead Museum; Kathy Skelly, Peabody Museum, Harvard University; John Grimes, Peabody Museum of Salem; and Michael O'Hanlon, British Museum.

Most particularly, I would like to thank Ruth K. Seto, Ida Hayselden, Sherlin Niau, and Josephine Kelley for their very special interest in the project and their deep concern and support.

Mahalo to John Clark, who helped edit the text and gave much valuable advice, to my parents, Mr. and Mrs. Jack Paik, for their help, and to Mrs. Leland (Sunny) Cook for her constant support and patience. And especially to my husband Dan and my children Mary, Hannah, and Donald for their understanding and encouragement.

INTRODUCTION
Shells and Man

Shells are classified as mollusks. The word mollusk comes from the Greek word *mollis* which means "soft-bodied." In her book *Hawaiian Marine Shells* E. Alison Kay observed, "The mollusks are an ancient group, second only to the Arthropoda in age and numbers of species among recent animal phyla. They are among the most diverse of all animals in form, structure, and habitat." Mollusks, encompassing thousands of species, range in habitat from the polar regions to the tropics, and inhabit almost every terrestrial and aquatic terrain.

Shells have played an important role in many cultures. Prehistoric man gathered snails for food, the animals that inhabit their shells providing a good source of protein. The shells themselves were used as containers, tools, and utensils. In addition to the practical uses of shells, many cultures throughout the world used shells as ornaments and as accoutrements for religious ceremonies. In some societies highly prized shells were used as a form of currency or as valued trade items.

Anthropologists throughout the world have noted the many uses of shells in everyday life. With slight adaptations many shells can be turned into knives, scrapers, and tweezers. In Northern California certain Indian tribes used the California mussel shell *(Mytilus californiensis)* as a scraper to remove the fiber from lily leaves for plaiting. In the Tuamotu Islands the pounders for food preparation and the adzes and axes for land clearing and soil preparation all were fashioned from the giant clam shell *(Tridacna gigas)*. Fishhooks made from pearl shells have been collected from many of the Pacific island groups and from the west coast of North America. The same shells are still used as decorative inlays for bowls and canoe prows in the Solomon Islands.

Various American Indian tribes believed that possessing certain shells gave an individual spiritual power. The ancient Hohokam Indians from the Southwest made long and arduous trips to the Sea of Cortez to gather shells, for they believed that the shells had the power to attract rain clouds from the sea. The shells were carved with great skill and used for adornment as well as religious objects. Another example of the use of shells for religious matters was discovered at the Indian Burial Mounds in Cahokia, Illinois. Archaeologists from the University of Wisconsin uncovered the remains of a chief buried on a blanket made of 200,000 shell beads.

In many primitive societies shells were used as a form of currency. Perhaps the best example of shell currency is the money cowry *(Cypraea moneta)*. According to Safer and Gill in *Spirals From the Sea,* "The shiny yellow Money Cowrie and the Ring Cowrie *(C. annu-*

lus) have circulated as currency in more places in the world than any coin." The authors reported that in India these cowries were carried from Bengal over the Himalayas to China. In the thirteenth century Marco Polo observed the use of this shell as a valued item of trade.

In many societies the shape of a shell was altered before it was declared a currency, a process perhaps analogous to minting. On Malaita in the Solomon Islands, spiny oyster shells were first broken into smaller chips. Then holes were drilled through the chips. The doughnut-shaped chips were strung onto a cord and rolled over a coarse surface to sand down the rough edges and sides. The resulting cylindrical beads were called *sapi sapi*. One-fathom lengths of these shell beads were used in trade with other areas, for purchasing a bride, and to help finance certain wartime activities. In the mountainous highlands of New Guinea a highly valued crescent-shaped neck ornament is fashioned from a gold lip pearl shell *(Meleagrina)* and called *kina* shell. The ornaments are traded across hundreds of miles, from the ocean to the highlands, and are a symbol of the wearer's wealth and status.

In some Pacific island societies shells indicated the wearer's rank in the social hierarchy and therefore became insignia of power and position. In Fiji the rare and showy golden cowry *(Cypraea aurantium)* was worn at important ceremonies only by the high chiefs. In other island societies shells were presented as gifts to solidify relationships between groups of people and to encourage trade with other commodities. In the Trobriand Islands, southeast of New Guinea, the Kula Ring was a trading system in which *kula* shell bracelets were exchanged within the island group for kula shell necklaces. This exchange was made only to enhance the relationships between the tribes. Other goods such as food or pottery were not allowed to change hands.

Before the arrival of Westerners, Hawaiians used shells primarily for implements and ornaments. The spine tip of the large triton *(Charonia tritonis)* or the helmet shell *(Cassis cornuta)* was filed off, allowing the shell to be used as a horn or trumpet in battle and for sounding alarms over long distances. A cowry *(Cypraea mauritiana)* that was a favorite food of octopus was fastened to a stone sinker and hook and lowered to the ocean bottom to lure octopus onto the hook. Fishhooks and scrapers were made from the mother-of-pearl, or *pā*, shell *(Ostraea)*. 'Opihi shells *(Helcioniscus axaratus)* had many uses, but were used primarily to scrape off the outer skin of the taro corm.

For decorative objects of personal adornment, the Hawaiians especially favored the colored feathers of certain birds, but according to Peter Buck in *Arts and Crafts of Hawaii*, they also commonly used the money cowry *(Cypraea moneta)*, the *kupe'e (Nerita polita)*, and several small species of the cone family. Buck also notes that "the small white shells of *Columbella varians*, popularly termed Niihau shells, were made into leis on Niihau."

HISTORY OF THE NI'IHAU SHELL LEI

Archaeological studies throughout the Hawaiian Islands have confirmed that shells were pierced for stringing and used as ornaments. For example, during excavations conducted by the Bishop Museum between 1958 and 1964 at Nualolo Kai on Kaua'i's north shore, scientists uncovered a piece of shell-work apparently similar to one described by Captain James Cook when he visited the island in 1778. According to the site report:

> A small armlet, probably made for a child, was found. Although the ends are damaged and incomplete, its overall length must have been about 160 mm, exclusive of ties. It consists of four parallel strands of *Columbella varians* Sowerby *(Pupu Ni'ihau)* shells, each about 8 mm long.
> Each shell is perforated by punching through the slightly flared lip, then strung on a cord and secured by half-hitches made with lateral cords on each side. The resulting strands of shells are joined by whipping, the cord passing back and forth between adjacent lateral cords of the strands of shells. The cord is two ply S-twist throughout, and is probably of *olonā (Touchardia latifolia)*.

During their visits in the Hawaiian Islands in 1778 and 1779, Captain Cook and members of his expedition recorded in detail their observations of the natural history of the islands and the life and customs of

---

A treasure of Ni'ihau shell leis cascading from a traditional Hawaiian calabash. Leis, courtesy of private collections; calabash, courtesy of Grove Farm Homestead Museum.

the native population. While the obvious social practices and rituals were described in great detail, ornaments received less attention unless they were particularly unusual and showy—like the feather work. Cook's observation of a shell ornament similar to the one unearthed by archaeologists at Nualolo Kai, Kauaʻi, is found in his journal dated February 17, 1778, Kauaʻi: "They also frequently wear on the head a kind of ornament of a finger's thickness or more, covered with red and yellow feathers, curiously varied, and tied behind; and on the arm, above the elbow, a kind of broad shell-work, grounded upon net-work."

David Samwell, the surgeon aboard the *Discovery* on Cook's expedition, also made an interesting observation of a shell ornament on Kauaʻi. He notes, "The women of Atowai wear necklaces of small shells and black seeds very curiously disposed, they also wear round blue stones on their breasts which they wet and make use of as looking glasses and they answer the purpose very well."

Cook's expedition collected a variety of objects from the islands and took them back to Europe. According to Adrienne Kaeppler in *Artificial Curiosities,* a catalog of an exhibit of artifacts collected on Cook's voyages, "It seems without a doubt that the early explorers and their crews collected and took back to Europe the different articles of curiosity, items of shell, feather, wood, etc. Indeed Europe at the time was anxious to see what these savage paradises had to offer."

One of the shell ornaments collected on Cook's voyages, now in the British Museum, is referred to in *Artificial Curiosities* as "Niihau shells." The shell necklace was identified and described by E. Alison Kay, malacologist at the University of Hawaii, on September 7, 1978,

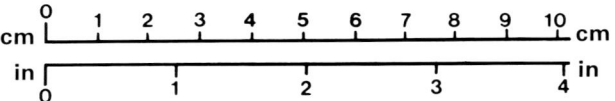

Left: *A shell armlet of Niʻihau shells found at Nualolo Kai on Kauaʻi's north shore during archaeological excavations conducted by the Bishop Museum. Courtesy of Bishop Museum.*

Opposite page: *A shell ornament of Niʻihau shells, predominantly kahelelani, collected during Captain Cook's visits in the Sandwich Islands. Courtesy of the Trustees of the British Museum.*

This formal portrait of Queen Kapiʻolani was taken in New York, May 1887, on her way to London to attend Queen Victoria's Jubilee. Kapiʻolani's formal Victorian dress is complemented by multiple strands of ivory-colored Niʻihau shell leis. Photo by Falk, New York City. Courtesy of Bishop Museum.

Queen Emma more than any other member of the Hawaiian royalty had a great appreciation for the traditional Hawaiian crafts. Her lively interest and encouragement were an inspiration to the islands' artisans, including the lei makers of Niʻihau.

Queen Emma is pictured here wearing multiple strands of ivory-colored Niʻihau shells. The individual strands are wrapped about the neck several times. Note the pearl clasp at the center of her throat, an indication that the Niʻihau shell lei was adapted to the style of the Victorian era. Courtesy of State of Hawaii Archives.

for purposes of an exhibit at the Bishop Museum: "Long lei with mostly red shells. All the small red shells are *Leptothyra verruca,* a small turbinid, but mixed in with them is one small, white *Turbo sandwichensis,* several small *Leptothyra candida* (dirty white), one specimen of a turrid, *Lionardia crassicostata.* The small, long white shells are *Zebina semi plicata,* a rissoid." The red shells, *Leptothyra verruca* are "Niʻihau" shells commonly known as kahelelani ʻulaʻula.

During his visits in the Hawaiian Islands, Cook made several visits to Niʻihau. His encounters with the natives were friendly, enabling him to replenish his ships' stores. Although it is not documented, it is very likely that the Niʻihau shell necklace in the British Museum was collected during one of the stops on Niʻihau by Cook's expedition.

Other early explorers in the Hawaiian Islands also noted the shells and shell devices worn by the native residents. During the late 1780s Captain George Dixon and Captain Nathaniel Portlock observed, "At the same islands are great plenty of beautiful shells such as Cypraea tigrina, C. mauritiana, C. talpa and others of that genus . . . and numberless pieces of the smaller kinds, of which last the natives form necklaces, bracelets, and other ornaments."

Between 1790 and 1795 Captain George Vancouver made three visits to the Sandwich Islands while undertaking the exploration of the northwest coast of America. During this period several Niʻihau-type shell necklaces were collected by G. G. Hewett, deputy surgeon on the voyage. These necklaces have been passed down through the years and are now in the British Museum along with those collected on Cook's voyages.

In his *History of the Hawaiian or Sandwich Islands,* James Jackson Jarves observed in 1843 in a description of hula dancers, "Their costumes were in conformity to their actions; garlands of flowers, necklaces of shells and leis, beautiful wreaths, fabricated from red or yellow feathers, encircled the limbs of the females."

The historical evidence found in the writings of the early visitors to the islands clearly indicates that a variety of land and sea shells were fashioned by the natives as ornaments. The manufacture of these ornaments was never limited to the island of Niʻihau, of course, but in the nineteenth century the practice of fashioning shells into intricate leis appears to have been unique to that island. In 1871 Queen Emma visited her home at Lāwaʻi, Kauaʻi and wrote to Mrs. Sara Weed, her friend and confidante in Honolulu, "Enclosed is a small necklace of shells, the latest novelty in that ornament from Niihau. I have only just got two strings of them." Mrs. Weed must have replied with a letter of appreciation to Emma for the necklace, and Emma in turn wrote, "I am glad you liked your necklace. It is a pretty improvement on the plain kind." In later years Queen Emma and Queen Kapiʻolani both had formal portraits taken wearing Niʻihau shell jewelry to complement their Victorian-style dresses. Emma especially was interested in the arts of her people, and it was this interest that undoubtedly helped to promote the popularity of Niʻihau shell leis.

Some of the finest observations of nineteenth-century life in Hawaiʻi were made by Isabella Bird, a traveler from Scotland, who visited the islands in 1873. In her book *Six Months in the Sandwich Islands,* Bird noted, "Niihau is famous for its very fine mats, and for the necklaces of shells six yards long, as well as for the extreme beauty and variety of the shells which are found there." In a letter dated April 8, 1873, Bird wrote to her sister in Scotland, "Mrs. Robinson is sending you a necklace only made on the island of Niihau, of four rows of shells. They are very pretty. I have two, a short and a long one."

So it seems that by the latter part of the 1800s most visitors to the Hawaiian Islands were familiar with Niʻihau and its beautiful shell leis. In 1888 M. Forsyth Grant, another island visitor, wrote this description of one of the exhibits in the Hawaiian National Museum: "A perfect model of a native grass hut quite small, but most exact in detail, was much admired, as were also the immense strings of tiny white shells, only found on Niihau and which formed a lei to be worn by royalty. Massed together, these shells have a curious appearance, and we were told that when Queen Emma was presented to Her Brittanic Majesty, her enormous necklace of Niihau shells created quite a sensation." The women of the royalty had quickly adapted the Niʻihau shell lei to Victorian jewelry styles by varying the length of the lei and adding a period clasp. The alterations in style elevated the appearance of the shell necklace so that it resembled a fashionable pearl necklace.

Because of the interest shown by visitors, Niʻihau shell leis eventually were offered for sale. An early reference to their appearance on the market is found in B. L. Finney's *Directory and Reference Book of the Hawaiian Islands 1896–97,* in which the author wrote the following about Niʻihau:

> Shells of great beauty and of many varieties are found upon the shore, and those with reddish, coral colored seed are strung into necklaces and similar ornaments are disposed to their fellow countrymen and to foreigners. Considerable taste and ingenuity are displayed in the manufacture of these pretty articles; and as tourists are, as a rule ready to pay liberally for curiosities, the natives derive a considerable income from their sales.

At the turn of the century Niʻihau shells were also strung in netlike curtains and then draped decoratively in doorways and over mantels. The Bishop Museum possesses a good example of a shell curtain that originally belonged to the Kapiʻolani Kalanianaʻole Collection.

By the twentieth century Niʻihau and its shell leis were firmly associated in the public mind. In one of his famous compositions, "Na Lei O Hawaii" (The Leis of Hawaiʻi), Charles E. King named each island and its representative flower. In one verse *pūpū* (shell) is given for

Ni'ihau along with the *hinahina* for Kaho'olawe and the *kauna'oa* for Lāna'i:

O Ni'ihau, Kaho'olawe, Lana'i	Ni'ihau, Kaho'olawe, (and) Lāna'i,
Ho'oheno me ka pūpū, ka hinahina, me ke kauna'oa,	You are decorated with the shells, the hinahina, and the kauna'oa,
Haina ia mai ana ka puana	Tell the refrain about
Na lei o Hawai'i, na lei o Hawai'i, e'o mai.	The leis of the Hawaiian Islands.

(Copyright Edward B. Marks Music Corporation)

For the people of Ni'ihau the shells were their flowers. The island is very arid and lacks enough rainfall to support the fragrant, colorful blossoms used to make the flower leis of which Hawaiians are so fond. Shell leis, therefore, were substituted for flower leis and were used to greet arriving friends, to wear to parties, and to wear while attending

Left: *Shell lei from the Bernice P. Bishop Collection, made prior to 1883 (from the possessions of Princess Ruth or Konia). Lei of five strands of off-white momi shells; graduated lengths of 18" to 25", fastened by an engraved gold clasp. Courtesy of Bishop Museum.*

Below: *Shell curtain used in an island home as decor at the turn of the century. From the Kapi'olani Kalaniana'ole Collection. Courtesy of Bishop Museum.*

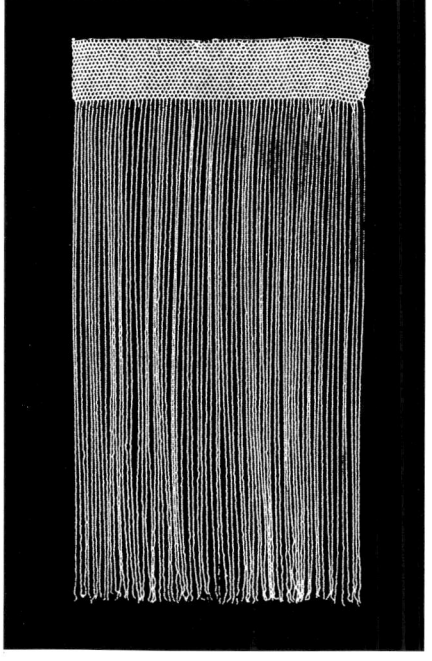

church services. Shell leis were also buried with the dead as a final gesture of aloha.

In the twentieth century Niʻihau shell leis continued to be sold. The 1922 volume of Thrum's *Hawaiian Annual* noted that "another long list of leis is shown in the variety of the sea and land shells and of seeds that may be found with the street vendors and at all curio stores. Shell leis for hat and neck wear and in long strands are frequently met with, confined principally to the variety of small beach and land shells, of which the rare white Niihau shells of the genus Columbella, and the iridescent Tasmanian shells of the Cantharidus genus, in long neck strands are favorites." The street vendors and curio shops in Honolulu that sold the shell leis bought them on Kauaʻi through relatives of the residents of Niʻihau. Retail outlets such as Grossman-Moody, Wichman & Co., and the Royal Hawaiian Hotel gift shop sold the leis primarily to tourists. Visitors purchased them not only because they were a permanent reminder of the flower leis of the islands, but also because they were a beautiful and unusual product of native craftsmanship.

On Kauaʻi, despite the island's proximity to Niʻihau, no retail stores carried the leis until the 1940s. Mrs. Juliet Rice Wichman of Kauaʻi recalls that the first Niʻihau shell lei she owned was given to her in 1932 by a visitor to the islands. It was a multistrand kahelelani ʻulaʻula lei that had been purchased in a gift shop at the Royal Hawaiian Hotel. Mrs. Wichman also remembers that her father, a prominent political figure during this era, was occasionally presented a Niʻihau shell lei along with the customary flower lei that was given at public speaking engagements. Just prior to the outbreak of World War II, Lihue Store became the first store on Kauaʻi to offer Niʻihau shell leis for sale. Mrs. Albert Duval, a *kamaʻāina* resident, bought her first lei there. She recalls that the leis were not very popular, but she liked them very much. In 1941 for $2.50 she purchased a momi kuaʻula shell lei with eight 50-inch strands strung in the Kui Pololei style.

During World War II thousands of civilians and service personnel were stationed in the islands to aid the war effort. They began buying shell leis as souvenirs and gifts, primarily single strands of the ivory-colored momi shells. The kahelelani and mixed-color leis were not very popular. A vendor who set up a seed and shell lei stand outside Lihue Store carried only the shorter Kipona style and the plain white single-strand leis. Her customers were primarily service personnel. My mother, Alice Morgan Paik, who was then an employee of the store, recalls that she had never before seen the wide variety of shells from Niʻihau that were in the vendor's Kipona-style leis.

During the war a number of servicemen were stationed on Niʻihau. While they were on the island, the people of Niʻihau sold, traded, and gave away many shell leis. The island-born soldiers returned home

A stunning array of leis from the 1940s. These leis were collected by Benjamin Paik who was stationed on Niʻihau during World War II. Courtesy of Mrs. Alice Paik.

with the leis to give to their wives, sweethearts, and families, finally bringing the leis to the attention of the local female population. Island women at this time, however, did not find many occasions on which they could wear these new leis. The standard of dress was then somewhat formal, and shell leis were not deemed suitable accessories for formal wear. The only island women who regularly wore them were the older Hawaiian women, who wore the white momi shells, strung singly in very long strands, loosely wrapped several times around the neck.

As the demand for Ni'ihau shell leis increased, the people of Ni'ihau began marketing them on O'ahu through relatives and friends. Parcels of shell leis were sent through the mail, or if someone went visiting, boxes of leis were hand-carried. The demand precipitated by the civilians and servicemen stationed in Hawai'i also resulted in two important developments. First, many new styles were developed that incorporated different and unusual combinations of shell varieties and shell colors. Second, the sale of leis became a substantial source of income for the Ni'ihau people.

Ironically, however, just as the shell lei industry was beginning to boom, it was dealt a nearly fatal blow. In an effort to prevent runaway inflation during the war, the Office of Price Administration was created to fix prices on all retail items—including Ni'ihau shell leis. The price of leis was so drastically reduced that production nearly came to a standstill, a major setback for the craft. The fixed prices did not begin to compensate for the time and painstaking effort involved in making the leis. As a result, only a handful of lei makers continued practicing their art. Despite attempts to have the restrictions lifted, they were enforced until the O.P.A. was abolished in 1947. Seeing the threat to Ni'ihau's business of lei making, and fearful that the craft would die, the Robinson family (who owned the island) personally took steps to market the leis for the people of Ni'ihau. On their trips to O'ahu they sold leis to Wichman & Co., Grossman-Moody, McInerny, and other well-known island stores that catered to wealthy islanders and visitors.

After World War II the lei-making industry was stimulated by a change in women's fashions; now "aloha attire," a more informal style of dress, became widely accepted. As women began wearing muumuus to parties and special events, they elected to complement their Hawaiian gowns with leis of seed or shell. Mrs. Masao Seto, a kama-'āina resident of Waimea and a retail businesswoman, recalls that she

---

Lei Kipona
Left to right: six-strand Lei Kipona, 36", six-strand Lei Kipona, 38", eight-strand Lei Kipona, 36".
A variety of leis from the 1950s, a period of rapid development and refinement in style and use of shells. Note especially the lei on the left; the momi are strung in the Single Pikake style, also called Kui 'Ōlepelepe. Courtesy of Mrs. Ida Hayselden, Mrs. Alice Paik.

bought her first Niʻihau shell lei in the mid-1940s from the late Mrs. Hannah Niau. It was a three-strand, pure white, Pikake-style lei, for which she paid $12.00. Mrs. Aletha Kaohi, a librarian at Waimea, recalls that she received a Niʻihau shell lei in 1948 as a high school graduation gift.

As the local demand increased during the 1950s, a concerted effort was made to sew leis of exceptional quality. Shells were painstakingly matched for size and color, and more interesting styles were created. The popularity of the leis increased substantially during the 1960s as many more women entered the job market. The Niʻihau shell lei increasingly gained acceptance among the working women because it was an attractive and enduring accessory to complement their island attire.

By 1965 Niʻihau shell leis were very popular and many of the better island stores carried them. The 1960s also was a boom decade for tourism, Hawaiʻi's attainment of statehood in 1959 having generated a tremendous amount of publicity for the islands. The substantial influx of visitors further stimulated the lei-making industry. Shorter leis became popular with the tourists because they were less expensive and more easily worn with dresses than the longer, traditional leis preferred by island women. Many leis dating from the 1800s to the 1920s were very long, often six feet in length, and usually consisted of ivory-colored momi shells strung singly. These leis were wound several times around the neck in graduated lengths. In the 1930s the colored kahelelani shells were used and the leis were shortened to 36 inches or less. The new Kipona style, with its mixture of shells, appeared in the 1940s. This style and the still shorter neck leis were very popular with the servicemen. During the 1940s came the Pikake style also, and today it is still the most popular with tourists and local residents.

During the late 1960s Niʻihau shells were made into bracelets and earrings as women wanted to complement their leis with matching shell accessories. The Lei Pikake was made into short lengths (6 to 8 inches) and fastened with a clasp for a bracelet. But shell bracelets have never been very popular because of the fragile nature of the shells.

Earrings of shell were made in two general styles: a rosette pattern of shells was glued onto metal earclips, or a small length of Lei Pikake, usually ¾ inch to 1½ inches, was attached to earclips. These two styles are still popular and have now been adapted for the pierced ear.

In the early 1970s additional interest in Niʻihau shell leis was

---

Lei Kahelelani
Kahelelani
Five strands, 18½"
A choker from the early 1950s showing a mixture of colors on each strand. During the forties and fifties the lei makers broke away from the tradition of stringing long lengths of ivory momi shells and introduced innovations in the use of shells and lengths of leis. Courtesy of Mrs. Ida Hayselden.

Niʻihau shell leis of all styles and colors are worn and cherished by island people, and their appreciation of the beauty and fine workmanship of this art form has passed on from one generation to another.

sparked by the *puka* shell craze. Throngs of island residents combed the beaches looking for puka shells (*Conus* sp.) to string into bracelets, anklets, and necklaces. The demand for puka shell jewelry became almost a national rage, and the finished products commanded very high prices. At the favored beaches there was hardly room to sit down, and competition for these worn-down cone shells was fierce. Prices eventually dropped with a flooded market, but the puka shell craze further established the acceptability of shells in jewelry and immediately elevated the status of the much more refined Niʻihau shell leis. As the demand for leis continued to rise, prices increased considerably. On Niʻihau almost all of the families on the island became actively involved in making shell leis.

On March 1, 1968, the *Honolulu Advertiser* reported that "members of the [State] House of Representatives yesterday formally adopted Aloha Wear for Fridays during the 1968 budget session. The resolution introduced by Majority Floor Leader Stanley I. Hara was one of several introduced yesterday." In pressing for passage of the measure, Hara had noted, "The wearing of gaily printed aloha dress is the symbol of our State's uniqueness." As a result of this resolution most working women wear muumuus to the office every Friday, and Niʻihau shell leis have become a stylish and popular accessory. Wearing a good quality Niʻihau shell lei is now a downtown Honolulu status symbol, and Aloha Friday is a day for island women to show off their island jewelry.

Niʻihau shell leis have become a standard fashion accessory among women in the Hawaiian Islands and are carried by most fine shops. Outstanding leis are treasured as valuable pieces of heirloom jewelry. The wives of Hawaiʻi's governors have traditionally taken a special personal interest in preserving and promoting island arts and crafts. Each first lady frequently appeared at state and social functions wearing a Niʻihau shell lei. Tourists also continue to spend liberally for these Hawaiian works of art. Many Japanese visitors in particular are well-informed, sophisticated consumers who include Niʻihau shell leis among their selected purchases. The Japanese are very partial to leis of pure white momi shells strung singly or in the Pikake style. The momi shells are like tiny pearls, a highly prized jewelry item among the Japanese, and so they pay liberally for the momi leis and do not hesitate to buy more than one.

The refined art of making Niʻihau shell leis is alive and thriving. According to Josephine Kelley, a young, talented lei maker, the majority of the people on Niʻihau are engaged in some aspect of the lei-making process, whether it is collecting, sorting, or sewing the shells. Many of the contemporary leis they produce are exquisite, fashioned in intricate styles and unique color combinations. The shell leis that long ago adorned Hawaiʻi's hula dancers and queens today adorn their descendants and many others who appreciate their beauty.

TYPES OF SHELLS USED IN NI'IHAU LEIS

Pūpū Ni'ihau

The three species of shells most commonly used in making Ni'ihau shell leis are *Euplica varians,* known as *momi; Mitrella margarita,* called *laiki* or rice shells; and *Leptothyra verruca,* known as *kahelelani.* These three species are commonly called *pūpū Ni'ihau* or *pūpū o Ni'ihau,* broad terms meaning, literally, "the shells of Ni'ihau." Pūpū Ni'ihau, however, are specifically identified with momi, laiki, and kahelelani.

The shells of all three species vary in color and pattern, some of the variability perhaps genetic, but some also determined by environment. While color and pattern differences occur in live-collected shells, additional subtle color variations develop as the shells are tumbled in surf and bleached by the sun. The Niihauans have names for all of these variations in color and pattern.

Momi

Momi, which means "pearl," are shells with the oval shape and often shining surface of their namesake. They are members of the molluscan family Columbellidae, known as the dove shells. Columbellid shells are quite remarkable for their enormous range of individual variation,

Lei Pikake
Pua melemele
Three strands, 36"
Pua melemele, meaning yellow flower, describes the warm yellow tones of this lei. Shells of this exact color are infrequently found. Courtesy of Mrs. Ruth K. Seto.

which has resulted in some complex species identification problems (Kay 1979). The scientific name of the species, *Euplica varians,* reflects that variation. The people of Niʻihau themselves recognize at least twenty different variants.

These shells are found throughout the Indo-west Pacific and are abundant in shallow waters on fringing reefs. The average length is about 10 mm.

Momi vary in color from pure white to dark brown and almost black. The darker shades of each color group seem to be found less frequently than the lighter shades. Shells of a light shade are referred to as *āhiehie,* meaning "faded"; those with darker markings are called *ikaika,* meaning "strong, powerful," or *ʻeleʻele,* which means "black." Shells with color intensities between faded and dark are described as *maikaʻi,* or "good." Shells that are light in shade may have been exposed on the beaches for a longer period of time than shells with dark color markings.

Descriptions of the various color forms of the momi follow.

Momi kuaʻula, "ribbed or grooved momi shell." These shells are off-white or ivory in color, sometimes with light brown streaks or blotches. They are the most commonly found of the momi group and are therefore the shells most often used in Niʻihau leis. Several variants

Variations of momi.
Top left to right:
Momi ʻōnikiniki, momi ʻōnikiniki ʻeleʻele
Momi kahakaha, momi keʻokeʻo
Momi uliuli, momi lenalena
Momi keʻokeʻo waha ʻeleʻele and waha ʻulaʻula, momi kuaʻula

Opposite page: *Lei Pikake*
Momi keʻokeʻo, momi kahakaha ikaika, momi lenalena ikaika, momi ʻōnikiniki ʻeleʻele, momi uliuli
Five strands, 46"
A classic example of a Lei Pikake arranged on a makaloa mat. Combining strands of the different colors of momi in this way is a favorite with lei makers. Courtesy of Mrs. Barbara Nishek.

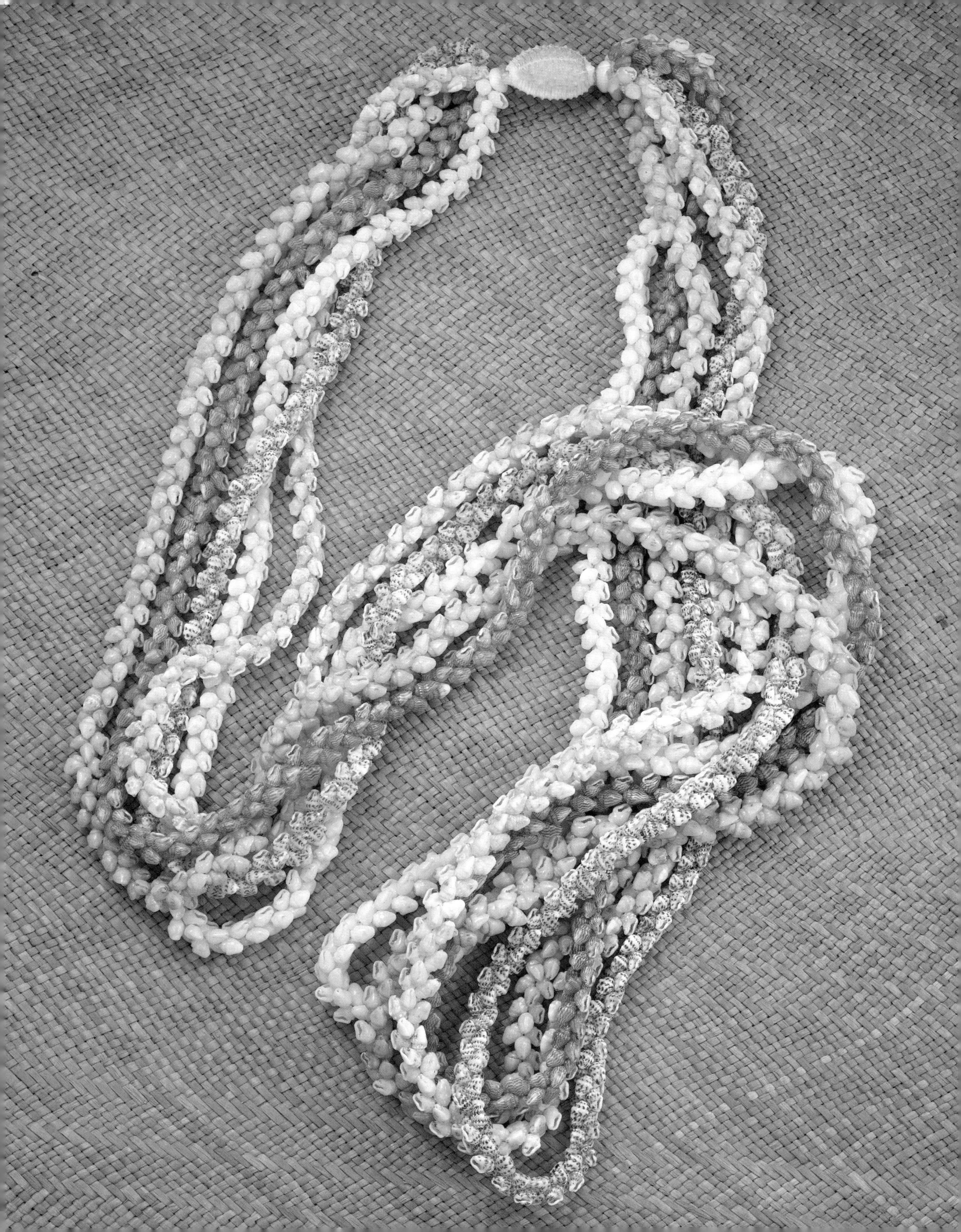

are recognized, all associated with differences in the color of the base of the shell: momi kuaʻula waha ʻulaʻula are off-white shells with a red base or mouth; momi kuaʻula waha ʻeleʻele are off-white shells with a black base or mouth. The Niihauans emphasize the spot at the base of the momi because this feature, when incorporated into a Pikake-style lei, is particularly attractive and desirable.

Momi lenalena, "yellow momi shell." These momi are a delicate shade of yellow and are the second most commonly seen variants. Those of a light or "faded" shade of yellow are called momi lenalena ʻāhiehie. Momi lenalena maikaʻi are shells of a medium shade of yellow, maikaʻi meaning "good, fine." Momi lenalena ʻeleʻele have black streaks and blotches. Shells with a rich, "strong," shade of yellow, called momi lenalena ikaika or pua melemele, "yellow flower," are infrequently found and are highly prized by lei makers. Shells with a pronounced dark spot at the base are called momi lenalena waha ʻeleʻele.

Momi keʻokeʻo, "white momi." These are pure white shells with no markings; they are sometimes called momi keʻokeʻo maikaʻi. A lei of momi keʻokeʻo is like a fine pearl necklace. Shells with colored basal spots are momi keʻokeʻo waha ʻulaʻula when the spot is red, and momi keʻokeʻo waha ʻeleʻele when the spot is black.

Momi ʻōnikiniki, "spotted momi." These momi have lineated spots of varying shades of brown, which spiral around the shell. Variants of momi ʻōnikiniki are momi ʻōnikiniki ʻāhiehie, with light brown spots; momi ʻōnikiniki maikaʻi, with medium brown spots; and momi ʻōnikiniki ikaika or momi ʻōnikiniki ʻeleʻele, with black spots. Momi ʻōnikiniki ʻeleʻele, which are found less frequently than the relatively abundant momi ʻōnikiniki ʻāhiehie, are classified separately from the other momi ʻōnikiniki by the Niihauans because of their distinctly characteristic black spots.

Momi uliuli, "dark momi." These shells are blue-gray with no markings. The descriptive term *uliuli* means "any dark color, including the deep blue of the sea." Because of the unusual coloration, there is some speculation that momi uliuli are fossil shells, and, indeed, they may be washed out from fossilized reefs along the shoreline. There are three variants of momi uliuli: momi uliuli ʻāhiehie, which are light gray; momi uliuli maikaʻi, which are medium gray-blue; and momi uliuli ikaika or momi uliuli ʻeleʻele, the most uncommon, which are dark grayish blue.

Lei Pikake
Momi keʻokeʻo
Three strands, 36"
Momi keʻokeʻo have the color and luster of fine pearls. Here the shells are graduated in size and the lei is especially well made as evidenced by the symmetrical arrangement of the shells. The cowry clasp was carefully selected for its color and size to enhance this outstanding example of a pure white Lei Pikake. Courtesy of Mrs. Ruth K. Seto.

39

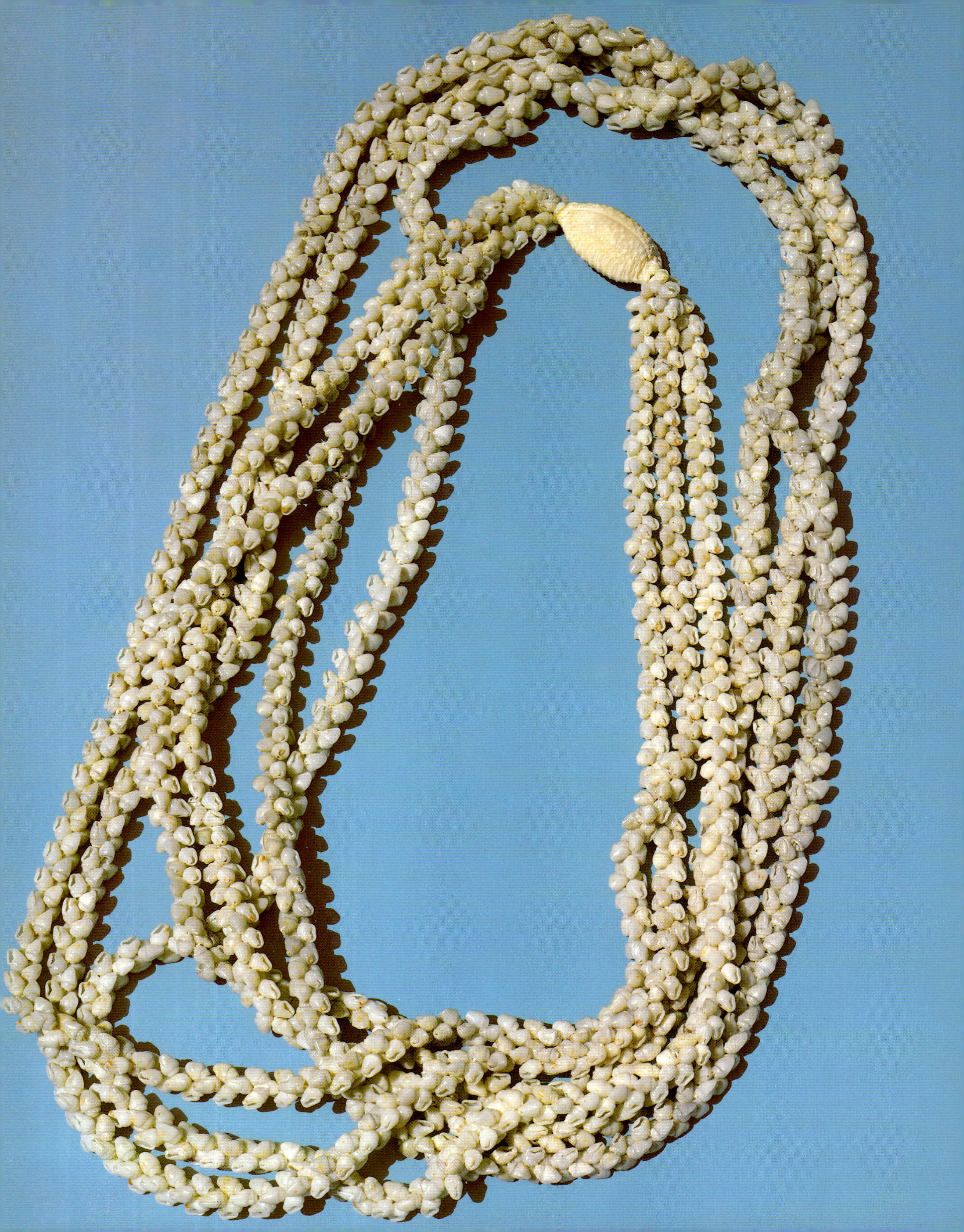

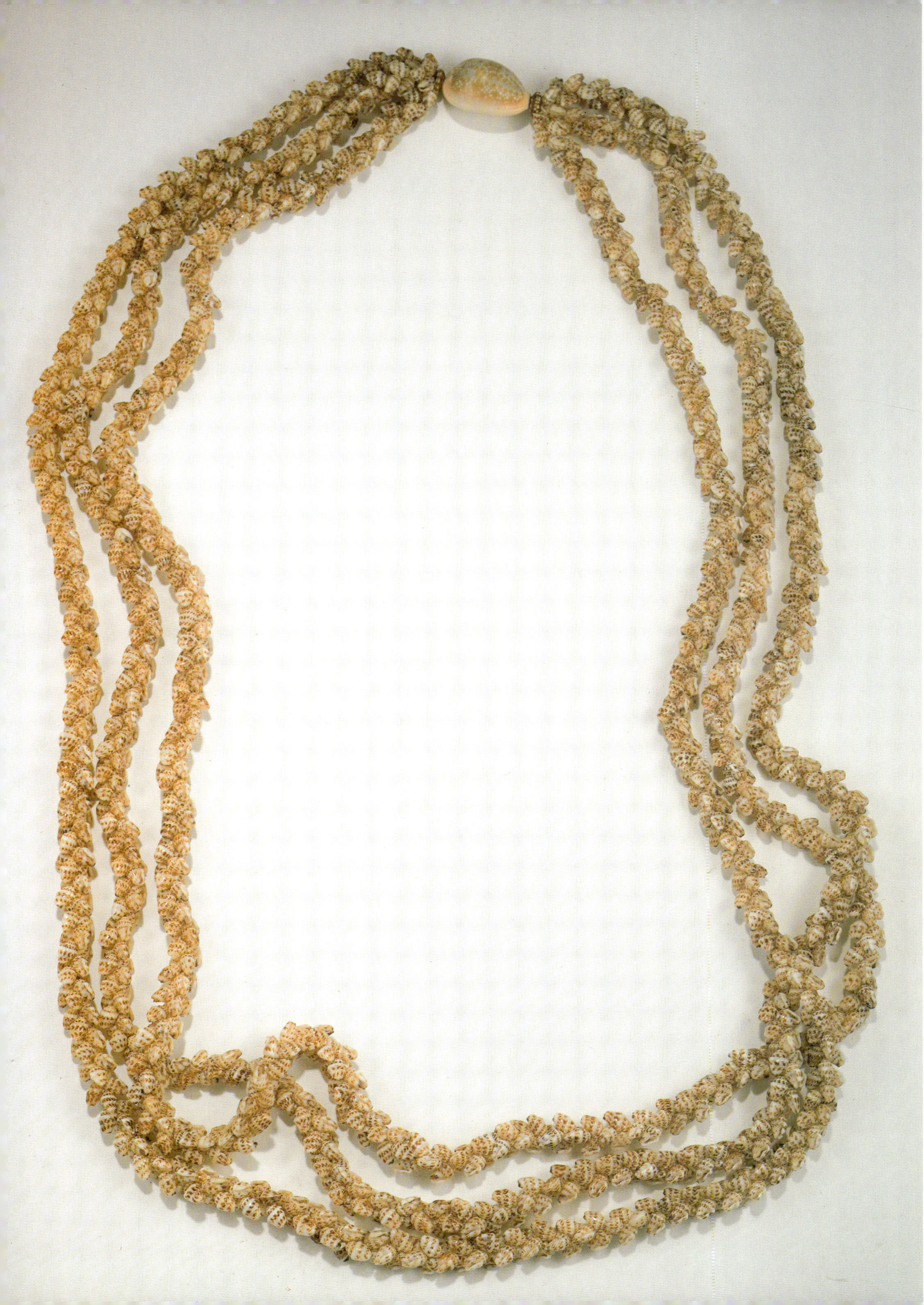

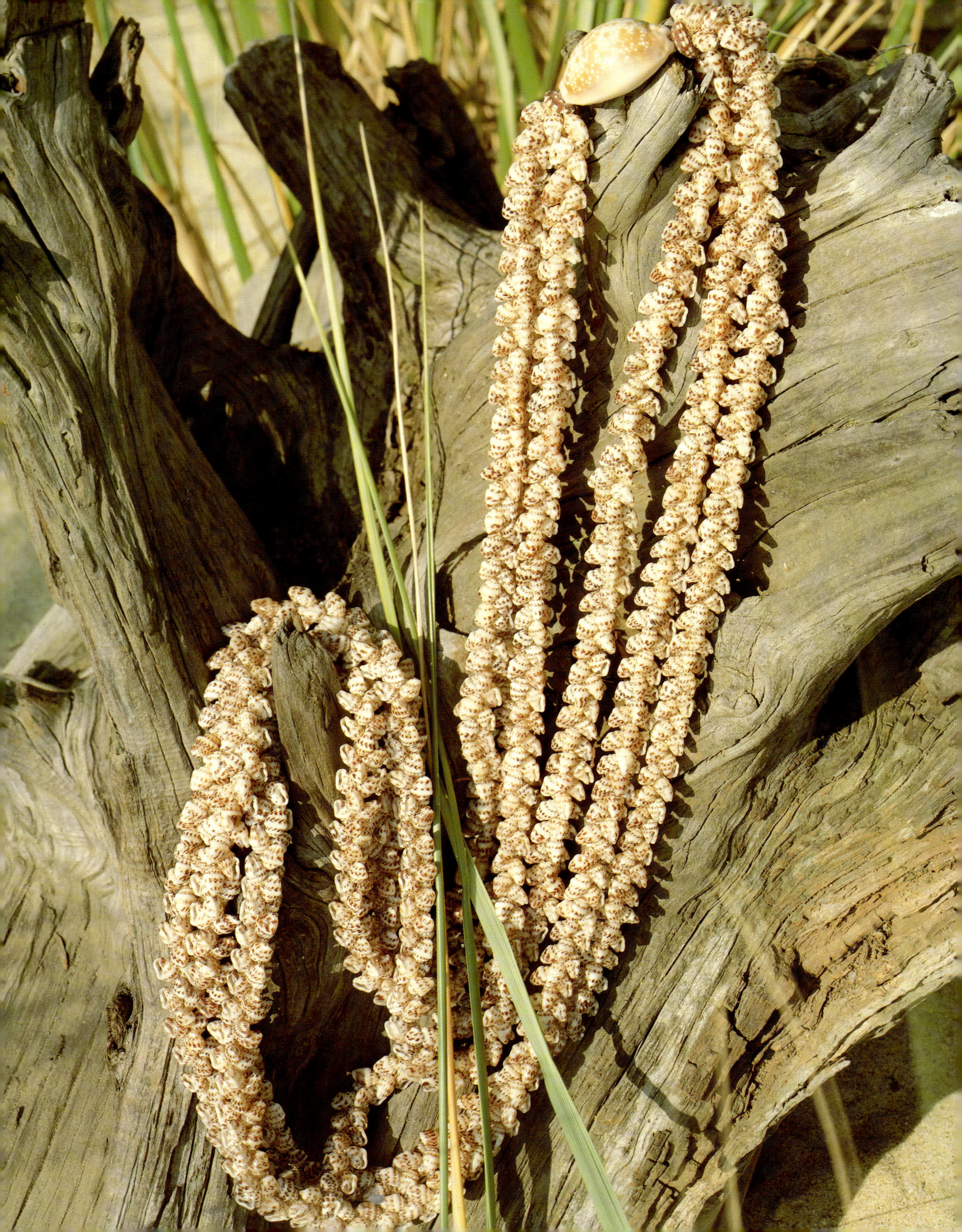

Momi kahakaha, "striped momi." These shells are honey colored with small, dark stripes running vertically down the shell. The stripes are most pronounced on the darkest shells, less prominent on light-colored ones. The variants of momi kahakaha are momi kahakaha ʻāhiehie, with light brown stripes; momi kahakaha ʻulaʻula, which have medium reddish brown stripes; and momi kahakaha ikaika or momi kahakaha ʻeleʻele, the rarest of the momi shells, with dark brown-black stripes. It takes a lei maker a whole year or more to collect enough momi kahakaha ʻeleʻele shells to make one strand of a 36-inch Double Pikake-style lei.

Laiki

Laiki, or rice shells, resemble grains of rice. Laiki is the Hawaiian way of saying the English word "rice." Like the momi, these shells are columbellids, found throughout the Indo-west Pacific and common in shallow water on fringing reefs. The species name is *Mitrella margarita.* An individual shell measures about 9 mm in length and 5 mm in diameter.

Laiki are usually ivory in color, often with yellow and light brown striations. There are three variants: laiki keʻokeʻo, pure white shells with no markings; laiki kua ʻula, off-white shells with light markings; and laiki lenalena, yellowish beige shells with brown markings.

These lovely shells, especially laiki keʻokeʻo, are used in many of the traditional wedding leis, for they are glossy and have a luster like that of pearls. They are usually strung singly (Kui Pololei), as the shell is relatively thick and difficult to pierce.

Kahelelani

Kahelelani, "the royal going," were perhaps so named because in early times they were used by chiefs. Kahelelani also was the name of an ancient chief. These are the smallest of the shells used for Niʻihau leis; they are therefore the most difficult to collect, pierce, and string, and the leis are thus the most expensive of all Niʻihau shell leis.

Kahelelani are small turban shells, *Leptothyra verruca,* members of the family Turbinidae. They are found in the western Pacific from

---

Page 40: *Lei Pikake*
Momi uliuli ikaika
Three strands, 64"
The momi uliuli, blue-gray in color, is believed to be a fossilized shell washed out from prehistoric reefs along the shore line. Courtesy of Mrs. Miriam Pahulehua

Page 41: *Lei Pikake*
Momi ʻōnikiniki ʻeleʻele
Three strands, 36"
Author's collection.

Opposite page: *Lei Pikake*
Momi ʻōnikiniki
Three strands, 36"
Author's collection.

Above: *Variations of kahelelani.*
Top left to right:
Row 1. *Kahelelani ʻeleʻele, kamoa, kahelelani ʻulaʻula, kahelelani keʻokeʻo.*
Row 2. *Kahelelani ʻākala pua, kahelelani mākuʻe, kahelelani ōmaʻomaʻo, kahelelani ʻākala ikaika (waipāpipi).*

Left: *Lei Pikake*
Momi kahakaha ikaika
Five strands graduated: 60", 62", 64", 66", 68"
Momi kahakaha are the rarest of the momi shells, the very dark shades (ikaika) being particularly rare. The beauty of this lei is enhanced by the background of a fine makaloa (Cyperus laevigatus) mat from Niʻihau. Historically, Niʻihau was known both for its shell leis and for these fine mats. Lei, courtesy of Mrs. Juliet Rice Wichman; mat, courtesy of Grove Farm Homestead Museum.

Opposite page: *Twenty strands, 60"*
A superb example of the traditional wedding lei of pūpū laiki. The exceptionally small shells were collected and strung by Mrs. Sherlin Niau Beniamina for her wedding. This unusual lei consists of 6,000 carefully selected shells. Courtesy of Mrs. Sherlin Beniamina.

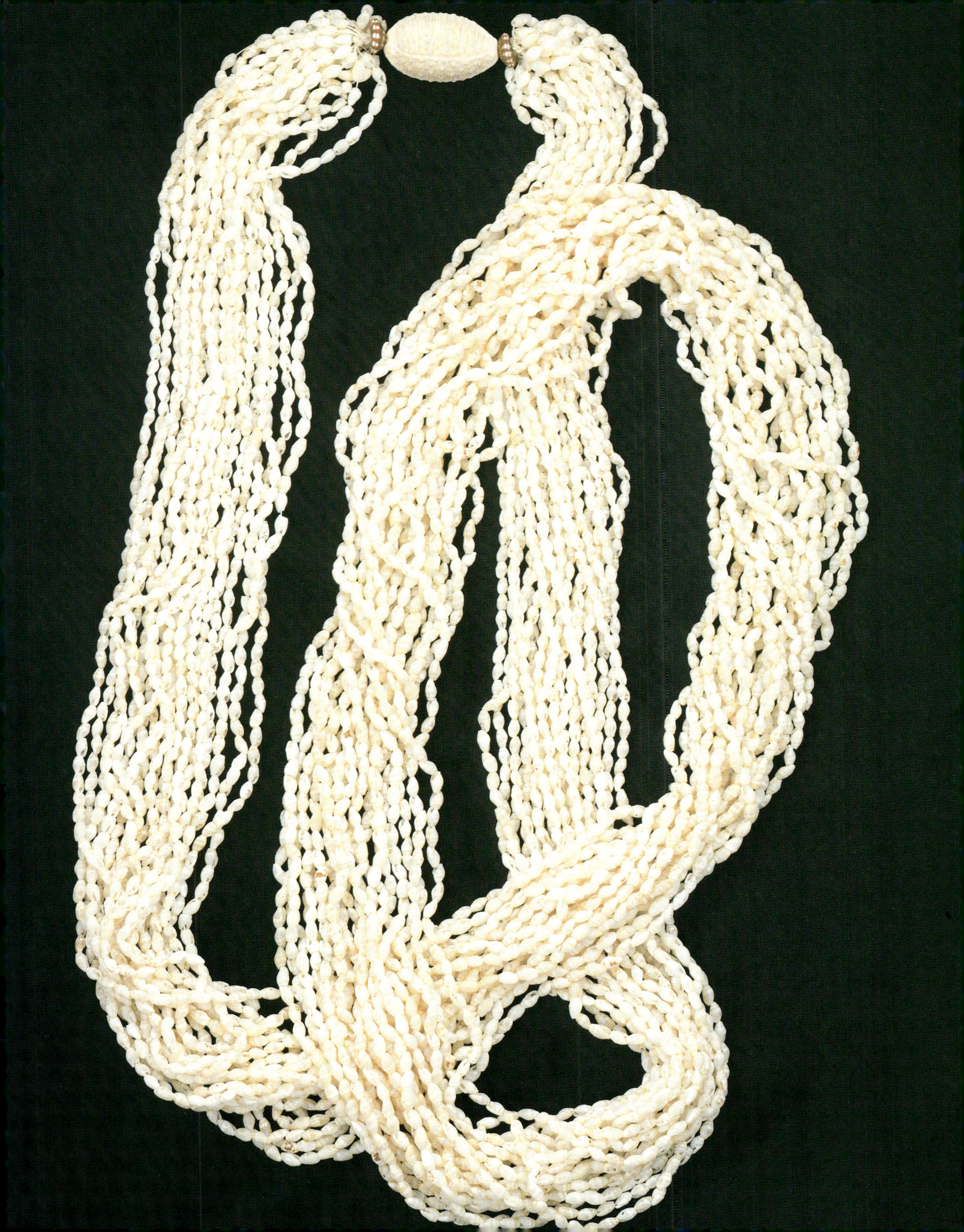

West Australia to the Marshall Islands and Hawai'i. These turbinids are abundant under rocks and rubble in tide pools and on fringing reefs and limestone "solution benches." The shells are about 5 mm in diameter and shaped like the rounded head of a pin.

As with the momi, the many variants of kahelelani are named by the Niihauans according to subtle differences in shell color and pattern. The variants include:

Kahelelani 'ula'ula. These dark red-burgundy-colored shells with no pronounced markings are rather commonly found.

Kahelelani 'ākala pua, "pink flower kahelelani." The shells are pink with circular bands of darker pink checks. Some Niihauans differentiate a pink-colored shell with light striations as kahelelani 'ākala pua 'āhiehie (light pink flower) and the darker-striated shell as kahelelani 'ākala pua ikaika.

Kahelelani 'ākala ikaika, "strong pink kahelelani." These shells are sometimes called waipāpipi, the name of the bright, "hot" pink blossoms of the prickly pear, *Opuntia megacantha,* which grows on Ni'ihau. The cactus was an early introduction and is grown as a barrier to contain the cattle. Waipāpipi is the rarest of the kahelelani; the price per strand of a lei is about three times that of leis of the other colors.

Kahelelani 'ōma'oma'o, "green kahelelani." These shells are light brown, striated, and with a tint of green. The green color is subtle, not usually apparent until several shells are massed together in a lei.

Kahelelani māku'e, "brown kahelelani." The name describes well the brown shells used in leis.

Kahelelani 'ele'ele, "black kahelelani." The shells are dark brown to almost black in color. To the untrained eye, it is sometimes difficult to differentiate between kahelelani 'ele'ele and kahelelani māku'e.

Kahelelani ke'oke'o, "white kahelelani." Though called white, the shells are pale ivory with a circular band of light pink striations. This is one of the most common of the kahelelani.

Other Shells Used for Leis

Kamoa

A fourth shell commonly used in Ni'ihau lei making is the turban shell *Turbo sandwicensis.* Kamoa is the Hawaiian word for Samoa, and it is possible that the name was given to their shell when similarly shaped small yellow land shells were imported from the South Pacific in the 1940s and sold in curio shops in Hawai'i. Another explanation is sug-

---

Lei Kahelelani
Ten strands, 42"
A rainbow of shells displaying the range of colors of the kahelelani. The yellow strand is kamoa. Courtesy of Mrs. Barbara Nishek.

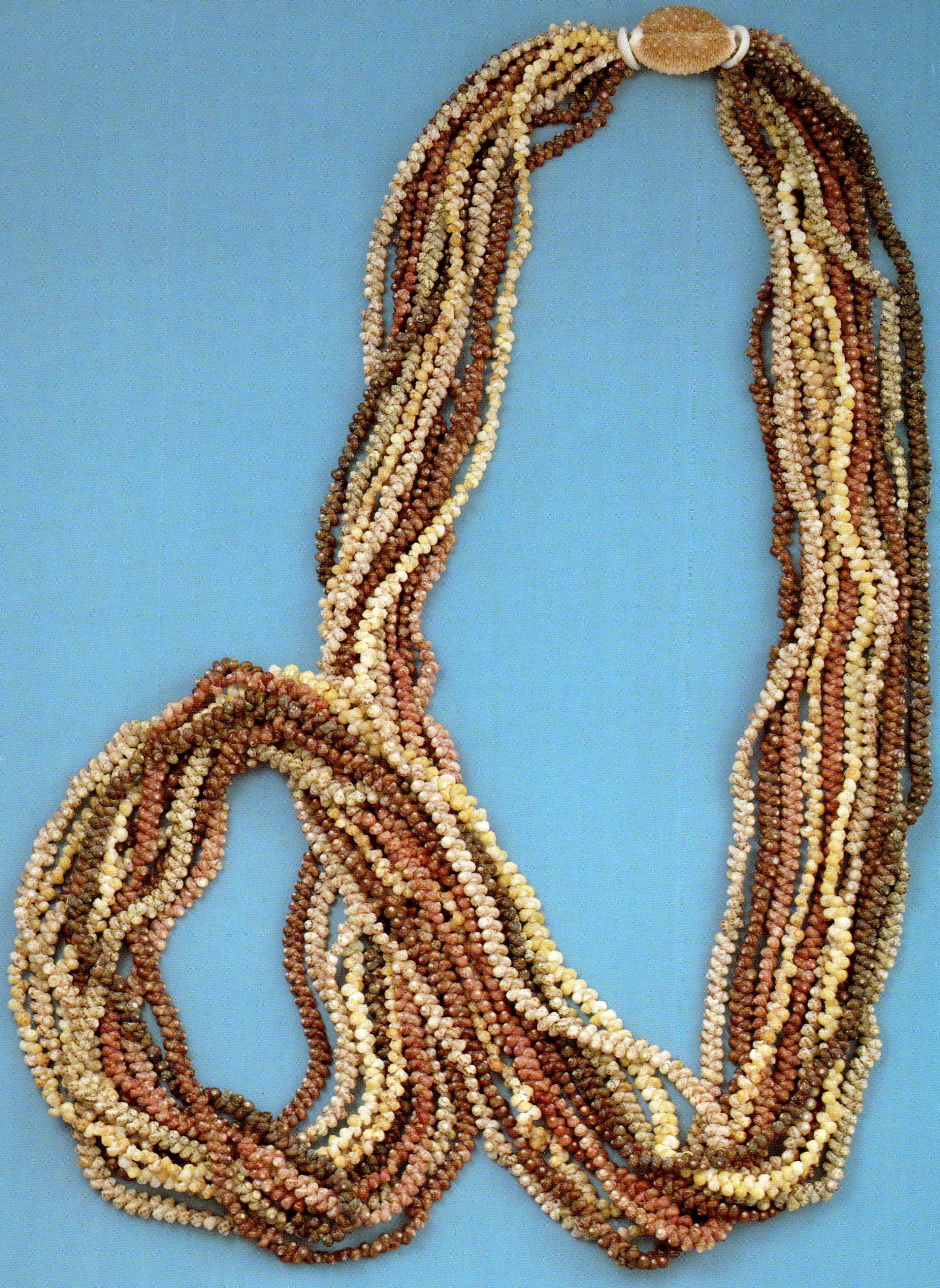

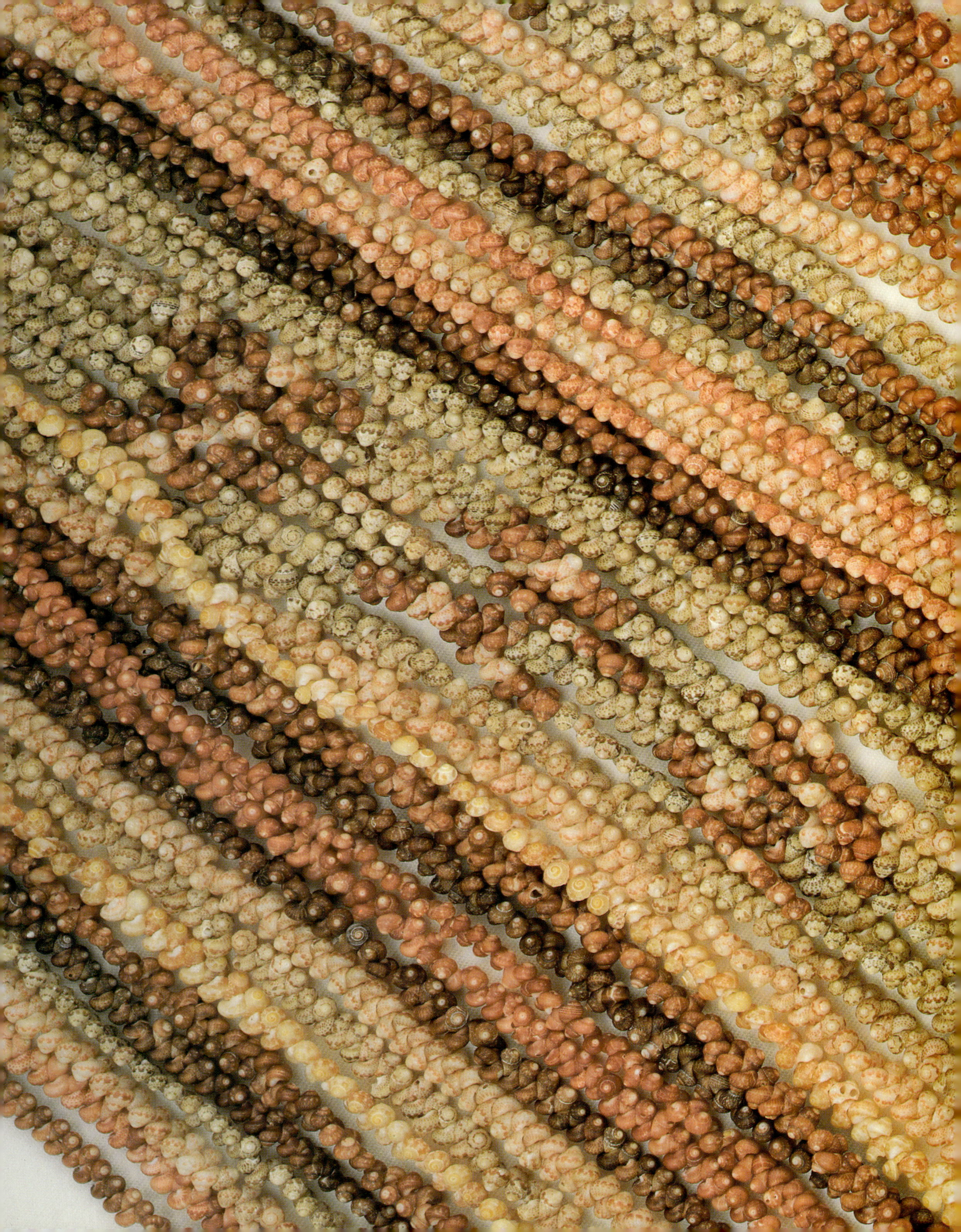

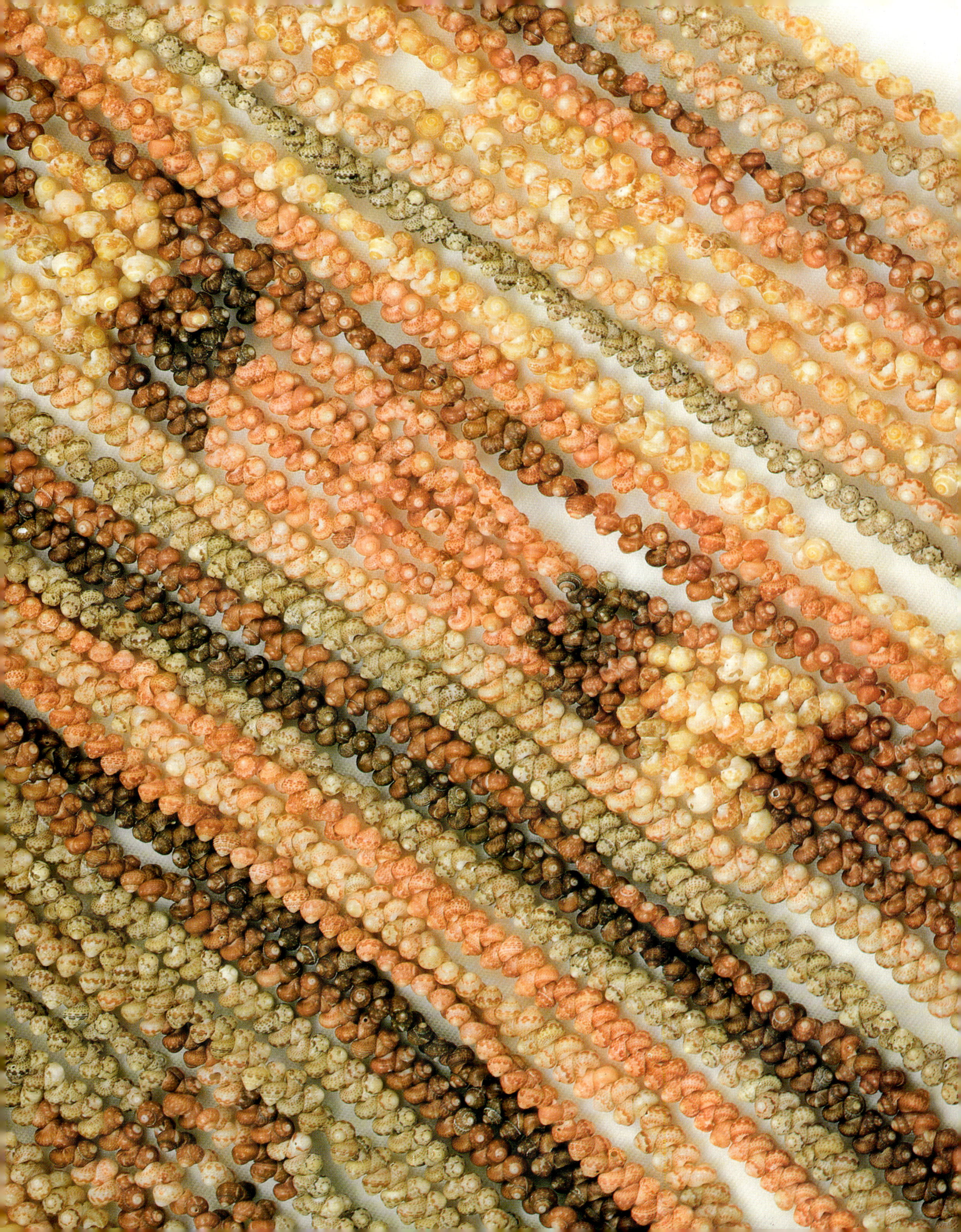

gested by Marie McDonald in her book, *Ka Lei:* "The spire tips resemble the yellow spores of the primitive plant called moa *(Psilotum nudum),* thus the name, Kamoa."

Kamoa, like kahelelani, is a member of the family Turbinidae. These shells, which may reach a length of more than 50 mm, are common in shallow waters shoreward of fringing reefs and on the outer edges of reefs. The shells are green or gray in color, with irregular flashes of darker green, black, and brown.

The Niihauans use the small juvenile shells in leis after clipping them down to the yellow tip. These small tips look like yellow kahelelani, and they are strung along with the variants of kahelelani.

Kamoa are sometimes referred to as hālili, which according to Pukui and Elbert are sundial shells. However, informants on Niʻihau refer to hālili as an older name for kamoa.

There are two variants in the color of the shell tip: kamoa hālili have lime green tips, and kamoa ʻili ʻalani, tips with an orange color. Both these color shades are uncommon and are used primarily as accents in a particularly fine lei.

Previous page: *Lei Kahelelani "Kahelelani was the name of an ancient ruler of the island of Niihau. The tiny seashell that is made into the finest lei on the island now bears the name of Kahelelani." (From ʻŌlelo Noʻeau by Mary Kawena Pukui.) Courtesy of Mrs. Ruth K. Seto.*

Left: *Lei Kahelelani Kahelelani ʻulaʻula Five strands, 36″ The kahelelani ʻulaʻula is one of the most commonly found of the kahelelani. This deep red color is a favorite of collectors. Courtesy of Mrs. Ruth K. Seto.*

Opposite page: *Lei Kahelelani Kahelelani ʻākala ikaika Five strands, 36″ A very rare lei of kahelelani ʻākala ikaika, sometimes called waipā-pipi. This shell variety, named after the hot pink blossom of the prickly pear* (Opuntia megacantha), *is the rarest of the kahelelani. Courtesy of Mrs. Jane Gilbert.*

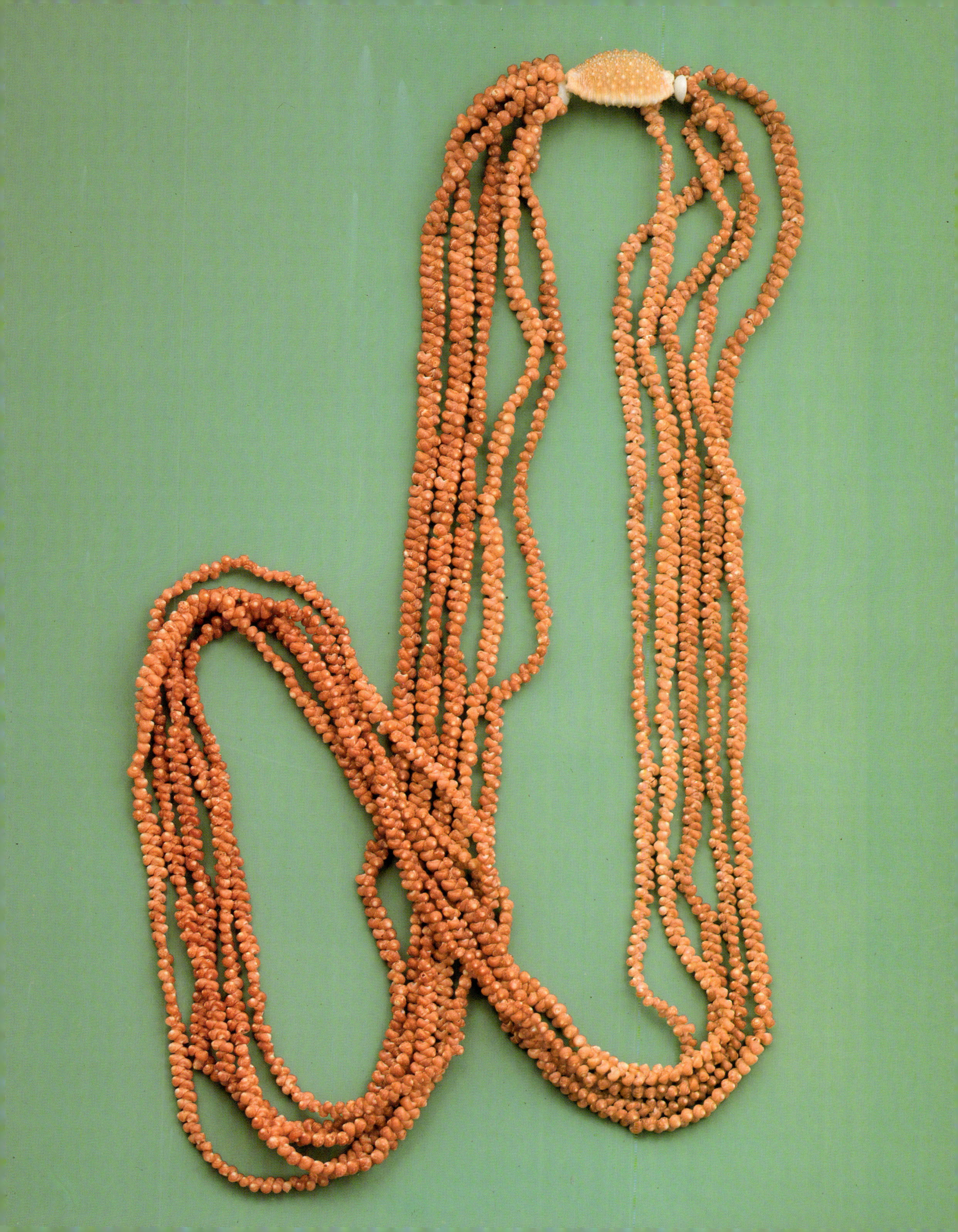

Less Commonly Used Shells

'Ālīlea (Strombus maculatus). This shell is known as the large dove shell because it closely resembles but is slightly larger than the momi or dove shell.

'Ālīlea are almost always strung in the Pikake and Rope styles because the shells are comparatively thick and are therefore heavier than other Ni'ihau shells. The leis are not made frequently because piercing is very difficult. The shells are strung on nylon monofilament fishing line, instead of the regular nylon thread, to support their weight. 'Ālīlea leis are heavy and bulky in appearance and are usually worn by men.

Pōleho (Melampus castaneus), "night cowry." Pōleho is also the name of a place on Ni'ihau. The shells measure approximately 13 mm in length. They are usually strung in the Pikake style, although occasionally they are combined with 'ālīlea of similar size in such a way as to give a two-colored, striped effect to a lei.

Laiki 'āpu'upu'u (Anachis miser), "bumpy laiki." This shell is also known as laiki nunui, "larger laiki," and the long rice shell. The color of this shell ranges from pure white and medium brown to light and dark brown spotted patterns. Laiki 'āpu'upu'u are strung like momi shells, but because they are larger, fewer shells are required for a lei.

'Ōlepe, "bivalve shell." 'Ōlepe is a general term used for all bivalves. On Ni'ihau, the 'ōlepe most commonly used for lei making has been *Chlamys irregularis.* These tiny pectens are thin and delicate and range in color from white to shades of orange and mauve. Today they are rarely used for leis on Ni'ihau, although the shells can still be found. During the early 1950s these shells were sewn into hat bands in the Kui Papa style. However, because a tremendous amount of skill is required to pierce and sew these very delicate, fragile shells and

Left: *Waipāpipi is named after the bright pink blossoms of this prickly pear.*

Opposite page: *Lei Kamoa Kamoa*
Five strands, 36"
Kamoa have the appearance of yellow kahelelani. Actually the juvenile form of the much larger kamoa has been clipped down to its yellow tip, and these tiny tips then strung like kahelelani. A pair of unclipped kamoa are strung on either side of the cowry closure. Circa 1950. Courtesy of Mrs. Ruth K. Seto.

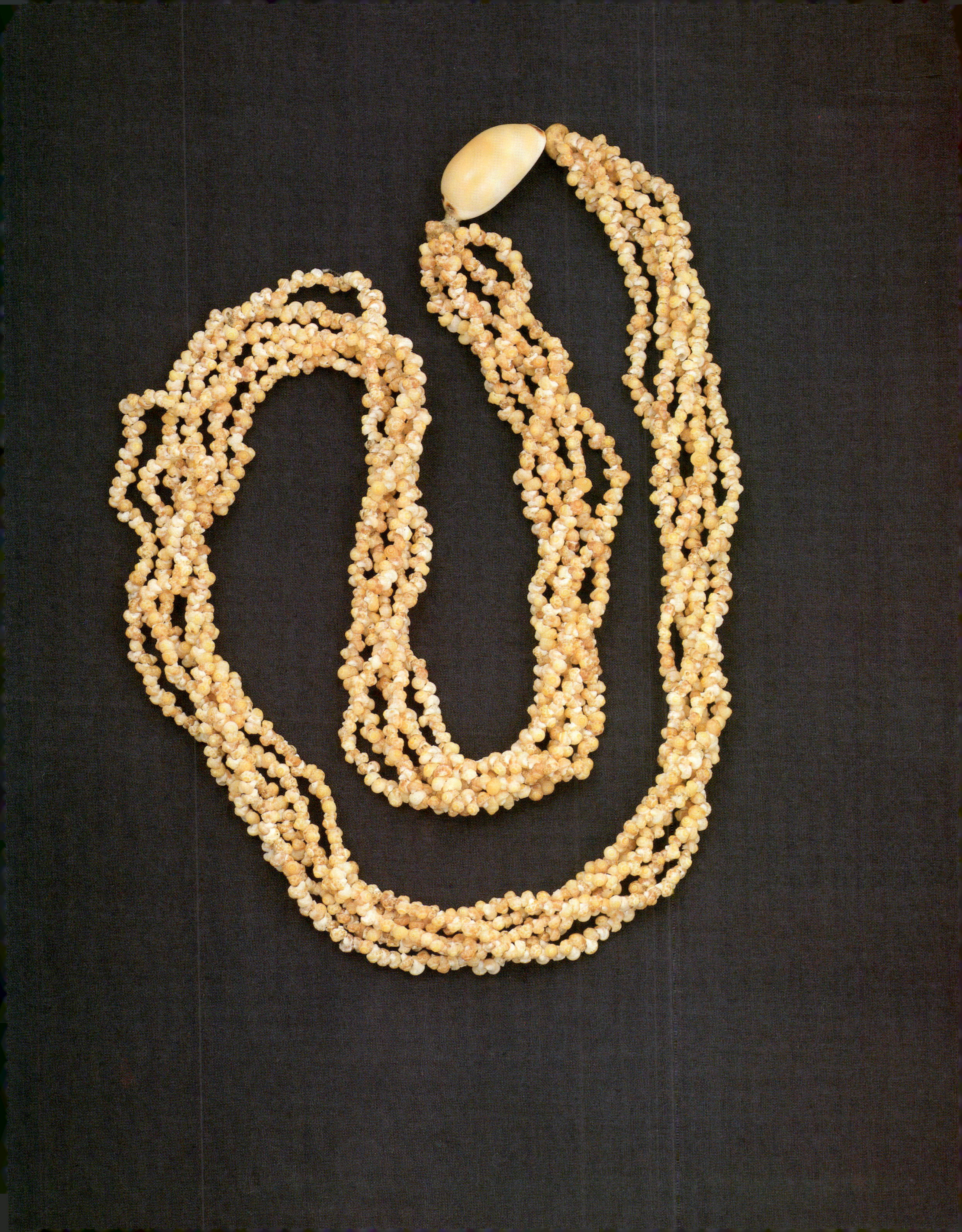

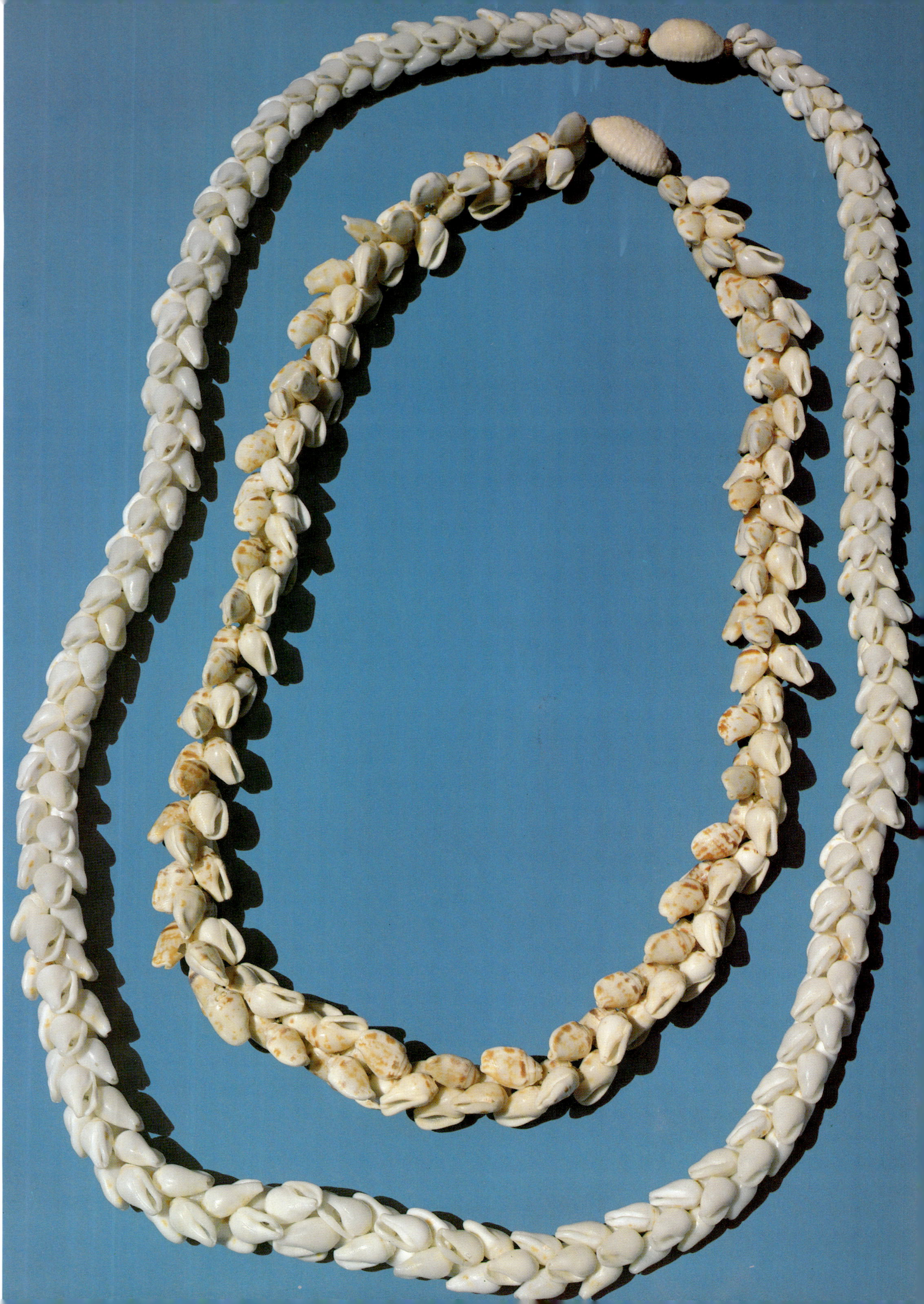

because hats that can support hat bands are seldom worn today, 'ōlepe lei making has almost died out.

Another 'ōlepe, *Haumea juddi,* was used for making hat bands during the same period. However, these shells, although also found on Ni'ihau, were more closely associated with lei making on the north shore of Kaua'i.

Shells Used to End the Leis

Kauno'o (Heliacus variegatus), are the shells traditionally used to finish off a lei. McDonald gives the definition of kauno'o as "scorched, partly consumed by fire, inflamed." They are also known as *pihi,* or "button," a general term used to describe the shape of the kauno'o and the puka shell. In color, kauno'o are variegated brown or black and white, and therefore are referred to by McDonald as the variegated sundial.

Traditionally, a kauno'o is strung at each end of a shell lei before the cowry, the joining shell, is attached. During the 1970s, however, lei makers began substituting metal barrel-type clasps and puka shells (*Conus* sp.) for the kauno'o, especially in the shorter leis.

Shells Used to Join the Leis

Ni'ihau shell leis are traditionally joined by a cowry shell (family Cypraeidae) between the kauno'o shells that end the lei. Pōleholeho, "night cowry," is the general term used by the people of Ni'ihau for all the varieties of cowry shells used to join the leis. Although most authorities use the word *leho* as the general term for cowries, other authorities say *leho* designates large cowries and *pōleho* (or *pōleholeho*) designates small ones.

Right: *Other shells used in Ni'ihau leis.*
Clockwise from top: 'ālīlea, laiki, laiki apu'upu'u, pōleho.

Opposite page: *Lei Pūpū 'Ālīlea*
'Ālīlea
Inside lei (spotted orange), 32"
Outside lei (white), 44"
Leis of 'ālīlea are heavy and bulky compared with the other, more delicate varieties of Ni'ihau shells. These leis are generally worn by the men of Ni'ihau on special occasions. Courtesy of Mrs. Ida Hayselden.

Above: *Lei Kipona*
Two strands, 62"
Kahelelani 'ākala pua with laiki āpu'upu'u (or laiki nunui). Courtesy of Mrs. Ruth K. Seto.

Right: *Lei Pōleho*
38"
This infrequently used shell is sewn in the Pikake style. Courtesy of Mrs. Ida Hayselden.

Opposite page:
Lei 'Ōlepe
Traditional 'ōlepe hatbands shown on a piece of pastel Hawaiian tapa. The last lei 'ōlepe was made in the 1960s. They are no longer made by the present generation of lei makers, although the shells are often collected. Leis, courtesy of Mrs. Juliet Rice Wichman, Mrs. Alice Paik, Mrs. Ida Hayselden; tapa, courtesy of Grove Farm Homestead Museum.

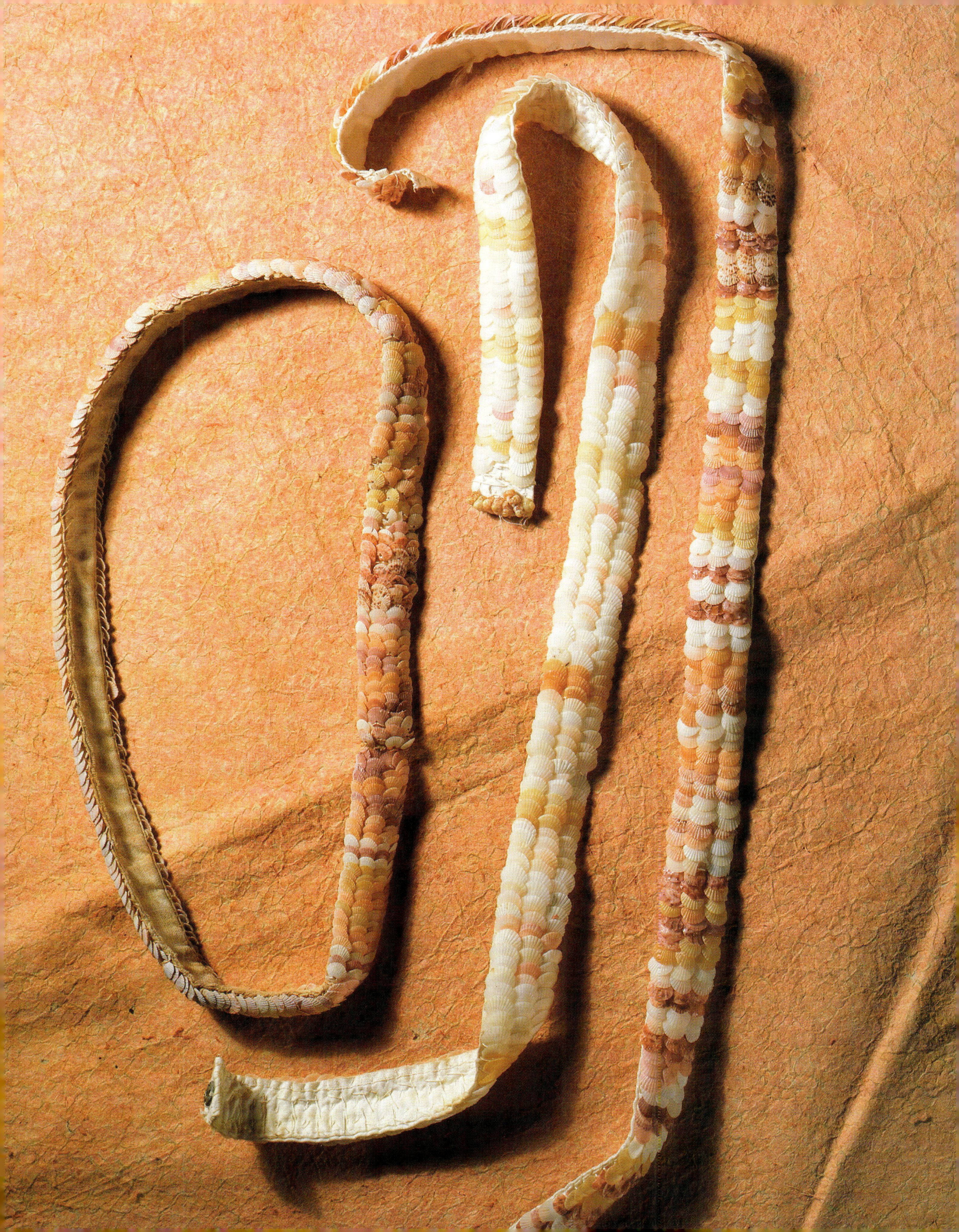

58

Some of the cowries and other shells used to end and join the lei.

Following pages: Close-up view of leis showing the cowry closure. The cowry and the accompanying sundial or puka shell are carefully chosen for color and size to complement the lei it is to join.

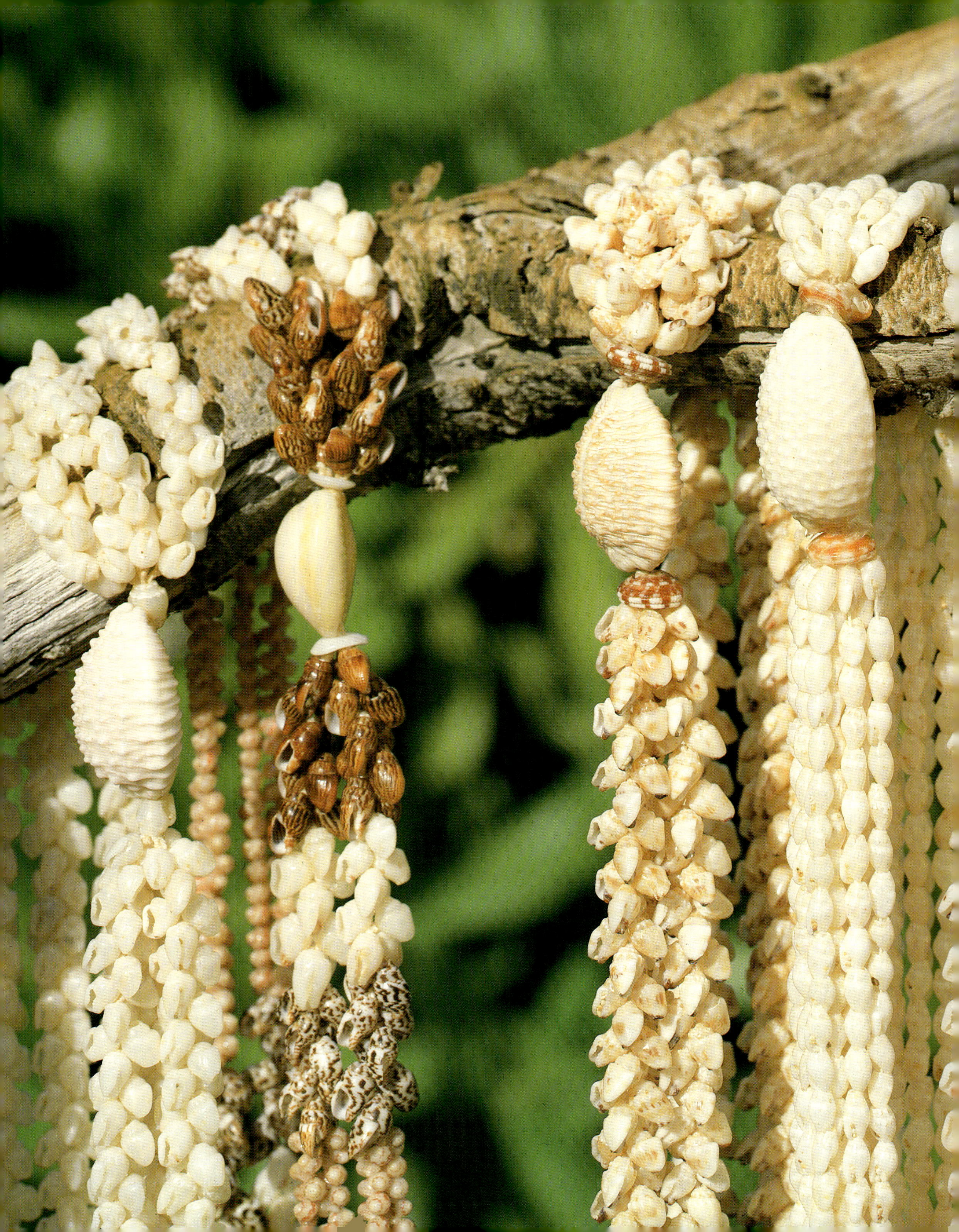

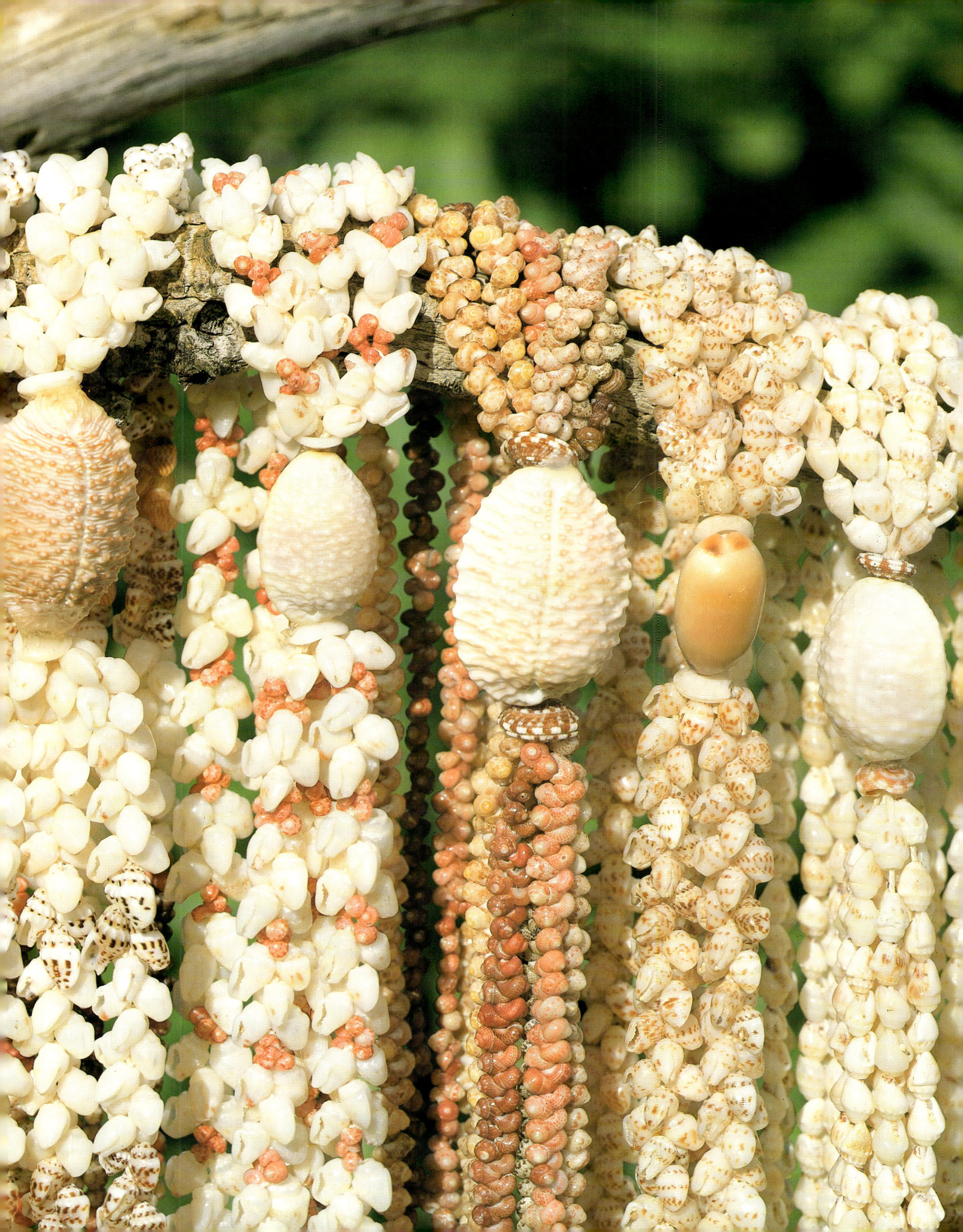

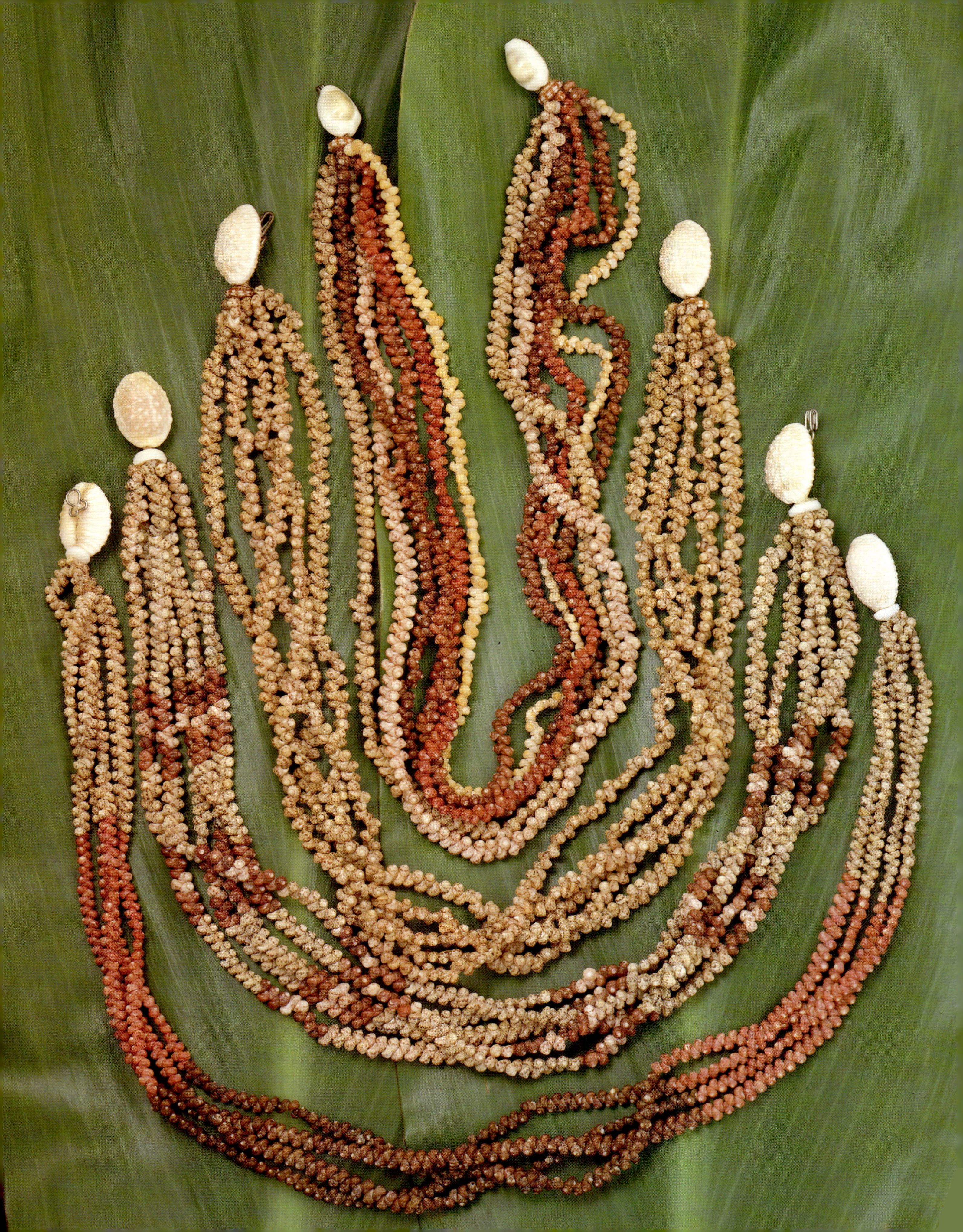

The cowry a lei maker selects for a lei must complement the color of the particular lei it is to join. For example, a lei of momi keʻokeʻo, the pure white momi shells, is joined with a pōleholeho ʻāpuʻupuʻu that is also pure white from prolonged bleaching by the sun; a lei of momi lenalena, the yellow momi shells, with a pōleholeho lenalena, which is yellowish brown; and a lei of mixed kahelelani shells, with an unbleached pōleholeho ʻāpuʻupuʻu or pōleholeho ʻakala, a flesh-colored cowry.

The size of the cowry must also be appropriate for the size of the particular lei that it is to join. The cowry's size is determined by the length of the lei and the number of strands it contains. A long lei, 50 or 60 inches in length with ten to twenty strands, is joined by a single large cowry, an adult of the species. A medium-length lei, approximately 36 inches long with three to ten strands depending on the style of the lei, is joined by an average-sized cowry. The small leis, those that do not slip easily over the head of the wearer, are usually joined by two small, matching cowries and by a hook-and-eye fastening attachment.

The cowries used in shell lei making are collected on the shore line where they have been exposed to the sun and the waves. Their colors vary directly with the length of time they have been subjected to the effects of the elements. Occasionally cowry shells not found in Hawaiian waters have been used to join Niʻihau shell leis. Such non-Hawaiian cowries as *Cypraea annulus* have been observed in leis made during the 1940s and 1950s, and more recently in the 1980s. Apparently these shells were obtained from leis imported from the Philippines or the South Pacific and sold in local gift shops.

The Niʻihau lei makers generally use the following cowries to join their leis:

Pōleholeho ʻāpuʻupuʻu (Cypraea granulata), "bumpy cowry"; also known as pōleholeho ʻakala, "pink cowry," for the unbleached specimen.

Pōleholeho ʻeleʻele (Cypraea caputserpentis), "black cowry"; also known as pōleholeho kupa, "native cowry."

Pōleholeho lenalena (Cypraea isabella), "yellow cowry"; also known as pōleholeho kūpeʻe lima, "bracelet cowry."

Pōleholeho puna (Cypraea moneta), "coral cowry"; also known as the white money cowry. This cowry can be smooth or bumpy.

Pōleholeho ʻōpule (Cypraea helvola), "variegated cowry."

Pōleholeho (Cypraea sulcidentata). No other descriptive name was found in common usage.

Lei Kahelelani
Kahelelani
Four leis, 18" to 20"
An array of kahelelani chokers showing various color combinations and the traditional use of the hook-and-eye closure for shorter leis. Courtesy of Mrs. Ruth K. Seto.

COLLECTING THE SHELLS

The people of Ni'ihau depend on the ocean for much of their livelihood. They fish, harvest seaweed, pick shellfish for food, and collect shells for shell leis. Because of the major importance the ocean plays in their lives, they are very sensitive to the weather and are always alert to any subtle changes in the ocean. The ocean conditions determine to a great extent what they are going to do for the day. When the ocean is calm, conditions will usually be good for picking shellfish such as *'opihi* or for harvesting seaweed. A slightly rougher day may produce conditions more suitable for throw-net fishing. When the ocean is extremely rough, precluding almost all other shoreline activities, the conditions are nearly ideal for collecting Ni'ihau shells.

Most of the Ni'ihau shells are gathered during the winter months, generally from October through March. During this period severe winter storms north of the Hawaiian Islands generate rough seas and high surf that deposit the shells in large quantities on the island's favored shell beaches. If the high surf continues into the spring, the collecting season is prolonged through May. The people of Ni'ihau make a concerted effort to collect while the shells are washing on-shore and to store as many shells as possible. Whatever they gather must last them until the following year's winter surf arrives once more. Kahelelani are the only shells that are also found during the summer months, but the ones collected during this period lack the luster of those found during the winter.

When the winter collecting season arrives, the people begin checking the debris lines on the shell-collecting beaches. Fishermen who

Collecting shells on the beach at Niʻihau, 1913. Photo by Herman von Holt. Courtesy of Topgallant Publishing Co.

frequent these areas make it a point to walk the beaches where the shells are found and watch carefully for major concentrations of shells. When a suitable volume of shells has accumulated onshore, the collectors begin their annual beach excursions.

The beach closest to the village of Puʻuwai is about one and a half miles away, and the farthest beach about nine miles away. Often one type of shell dominates on a particular beach; so collectors may decide in advance where to concentrate their efforts, depending on what they are seeking. At the most popular shell beach nearly all of the shell varieties may be found, while other beaches have various mixtures of shell types and colors.

To reach the shell beaches, the people walk the hot, dusty, unpaved roads, for there are no private motor vehicles on Niʻihau. In recent years, however, some of the more resourceful shell collectors have been riding bicycles over the unpaved roads. The island is extremely dry, with little vegetation to offer shade, and so every excursion to the beach means a full day in the sun.

On a day set aside for shell collecting, the collectors leave home very early in the morning, usually about 5:00 A.M., to avoid walking in the heat of the morning. They pack ample supplies of water and bring glass jars, cloth rice bags, and other containers to hold the shells. Food supplies, consisting primarily of crackers and cookies, are light-weight and kept to a minimum. This allows the collectors to carry as much water as they will need. They also bring hats and umbrellas for protection from the sun.

Shell collecting, besides being an economic pursuit, is a social affair. Families and friends travel together, laughing and talking as they walk to the beaches. Occasional stops are made along the way to rest and to drink water. After arriving at the beach, the collectors find a shady area under a tree or between several large rocks. There they store their water and other personal effects. The gallon-jug containers of water are buried in the sand to keep them cool. At the beaches where caves are found near the shore, the water containers are buried in the sand in the caves. Any water unused by the end of the day is stored in the caves as a reserve supply for future excursions to these isolated beaches.

Out on the sand the collectors walk along the debris line looking for a spot which from their experience they believe may be productive. If someone is already collecting near the site they like, they simply move farther along and select another suitable spot. There are no territories reserved for particular families or groups. Generally, the first one to arrive at the beach gets the prime collecting area.

When a favorable site has been selected, the collectors assume a comfortable sitting or lying position on the debris line where most of the shells have accumulated. Those with beach umbrellas secure them in the sand. The collectors then move slowly along the debris line, repositioning themselves each time they have finished combing a particular area. They collect all of the varieties of Ni'ihau shells that they find, including those used for joining the leis. All of the shells are placed in the same container; sorting takes place later back in the village.

While the collectors are gathering shells, they do little or no talking to each other. They concentrate totally on the task at hand, focusing their eyes only on the shells. They move their eyes very slowly, an inch at a time. The constant focusing necessary to discern such tiny objects coupled with the harsh, intense glare of the sun reflecting off the sand and the ocean's surface puts a tremendous strain on the eyes. The collectors periodically stop to rest their eyes from this tiresome work and to drink water, but throughout the course of the day they actually take few breaks.

Occasionally the collectors move from the debris line toward the water's edge, but often the high winter surf that sweeps across the beaches forces them back. All shell collecting, however, is done on land on the beaches. The people of Ni'ihau never search for live shell specimens. All of the shells collected for their leis have been vacated by the sea snails who once inhabited them.

The amount of time spent collecting shells depends on the volume of shells collected and the intensity of the sun. If shells are not abundant, the collectors go home after a few hours. If they are finding substantial amounts, some will stay well into the late afternoon. The most determined collectors tolerate the long hours in the hot sun for an entire day, but most of them are not able to endure the harsh exposure and leave after four or five hours. On exceptionally productive days the collectors make the most of this abundance by filling large cloth rice bags with sand skimmed from the debris line and carry them home. The sand is left to dry and then thoroughly searched at the convenience of the collector.

On an average day of collecting, one person may fill a small baby food jar and on a good day, a large 18-ounce guava jelly jar. The collectors pick only whole shells and discard any that are obviously broken or flawed, but momi or laiki shells with naturally worn tips are kept because they can be used.

The most industrious and productive collectors are the unmarried young women and the married women without large families. These people do most of the collecting because they are physically better able to walk the distances to and from the beaches and to spend long hours in the sun. Extended families on Niʻihau with many young women usually have a much larger supply of shells than other families. The older women generally spend their time sorting, piercing, and stringing the leis in the comfort of their homes. At one time or another, however, almost everyone on Niʻihau, including the children and the men, participates in collecting the shells that make such an important economic contribution to their lives.

When the shells are brought home, they are set out to dry in a shaded area for a day or two. After the brief drying period, they are placed in cloth bags or jars and stored for later use. The shells are never rinsed in fresh water for fear it will dull their luster. Sorting takes place later, as the shells are needed for leis, but during the winter months collecting is the activity of primary importance.

Some of the shells, sorted and unsorted, are sent along with food items such as fish and ʻopihi to relatives who live on Kauaʻi. The Kauaʻi relatives reciprocate by purchasing food items that are not available on Niʻihau and shipping them to the island. They also provide housing and other amenities to their Niʻihau relatives whenever they come to visit.

Contrary to popular belief, Niʻihau shells are found on the other Hawaiian islands as well as in other Pacific island groups, but the shells appear to occur in much greater abundance on Niʻihau and are of much better quality there than anywhere else. Niʻihau shells can be found on Kauaʻi's northern and northeastern beaches, for example, but these shells usually lack the luster and color range of those found on Niʻihau. In addition the Kauaʻi shells are often stained reddish brown, a discoloration probably caused by the eroded soil that is carried into the ocean by Kauaʻi's north shore rivers.

Figure B

MAKING A LEI

Before a Niʻihau shell lei is actually strung, the shells are sorted by types, colors, and sizes, and placed in scores of individual bottles and containers. Sorting is a time-consuming, never-ending process, but once the desired amount of a particular type of shell or shells is accumulated, the actual lei-making process begins.

The shells are prepared by first removing the grains of sand from the shell aperture with a sharp-pointed instrument, usually a stainless steel awl made from an umbrella spine or bicycle spoke. Then, depending on the style of lei to be made, a hole is pierced in a particular place on the shell by pushing very hard into the shell with a twisting, drill-like motion. Making the hole requires exactly the right amount of skillfully applied pressure. However, even with the great

Steps in Making a Lei Figure A
   A. *Supplies necessary for making a Niʻihau shell lei.*
   B. *Unsorted shells.*

Figure C

Figure D

C. Unsorted shells.
D & E. Sorting the shells by type, color, and size.

Figure E

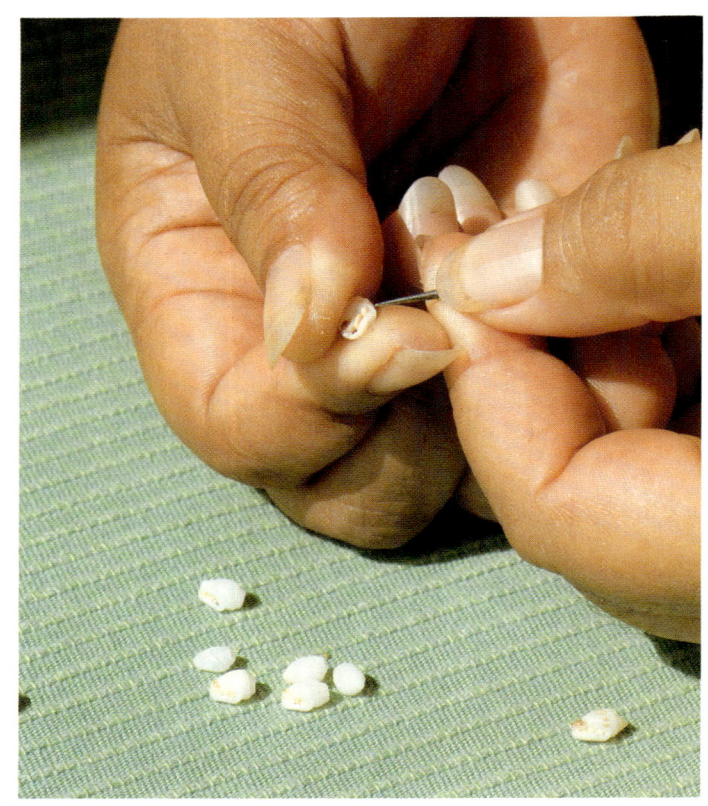

Figure F

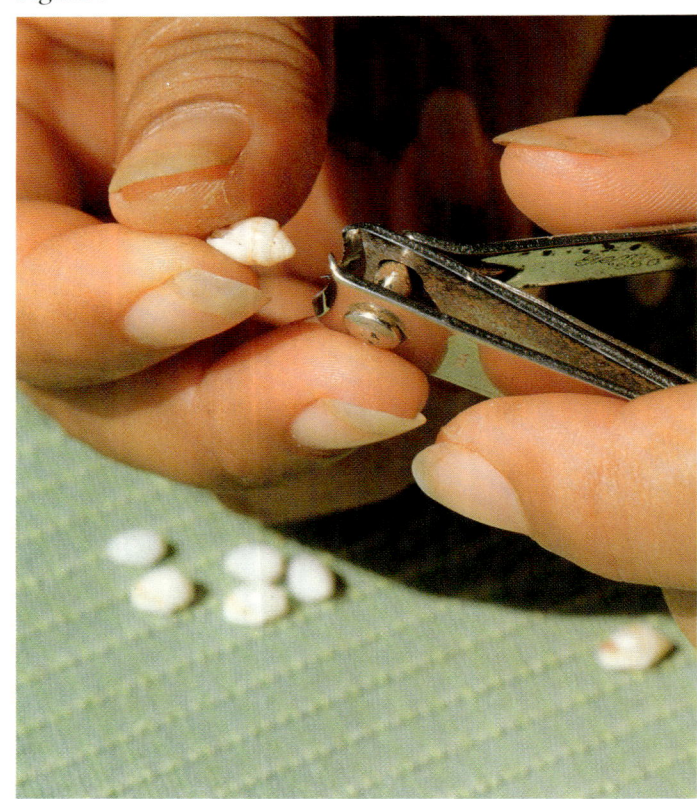

Figure G

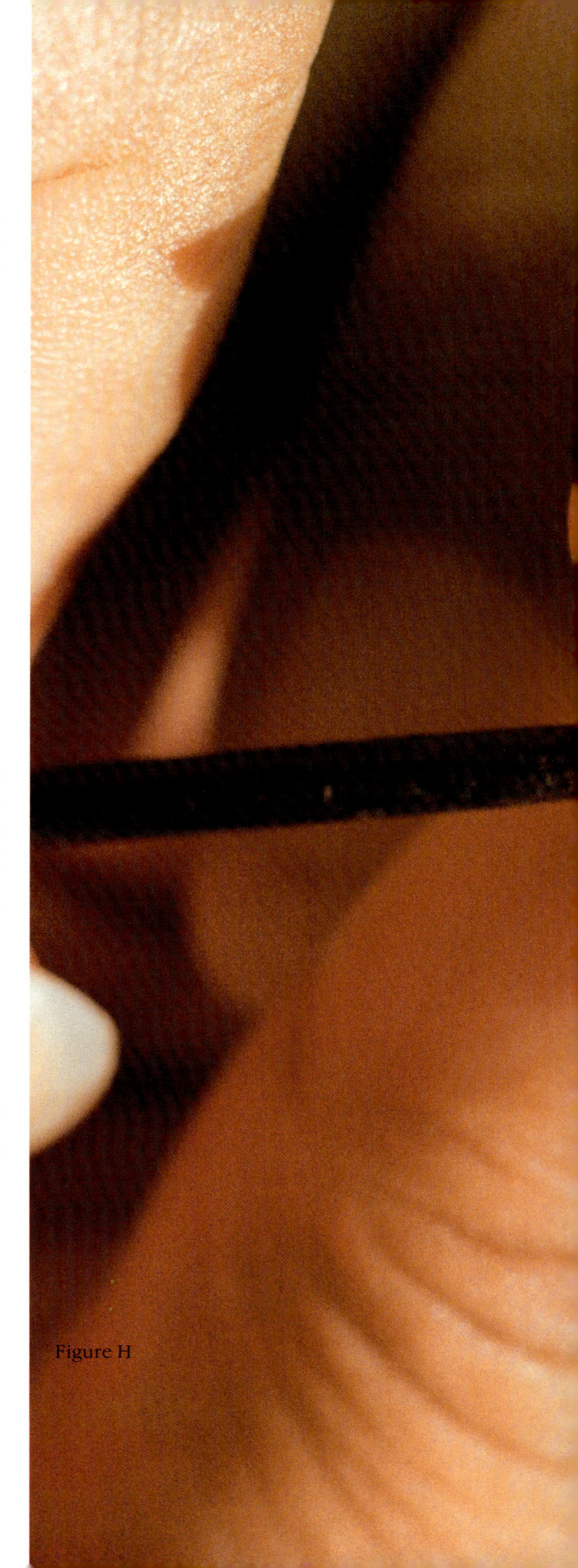

72

Figure H

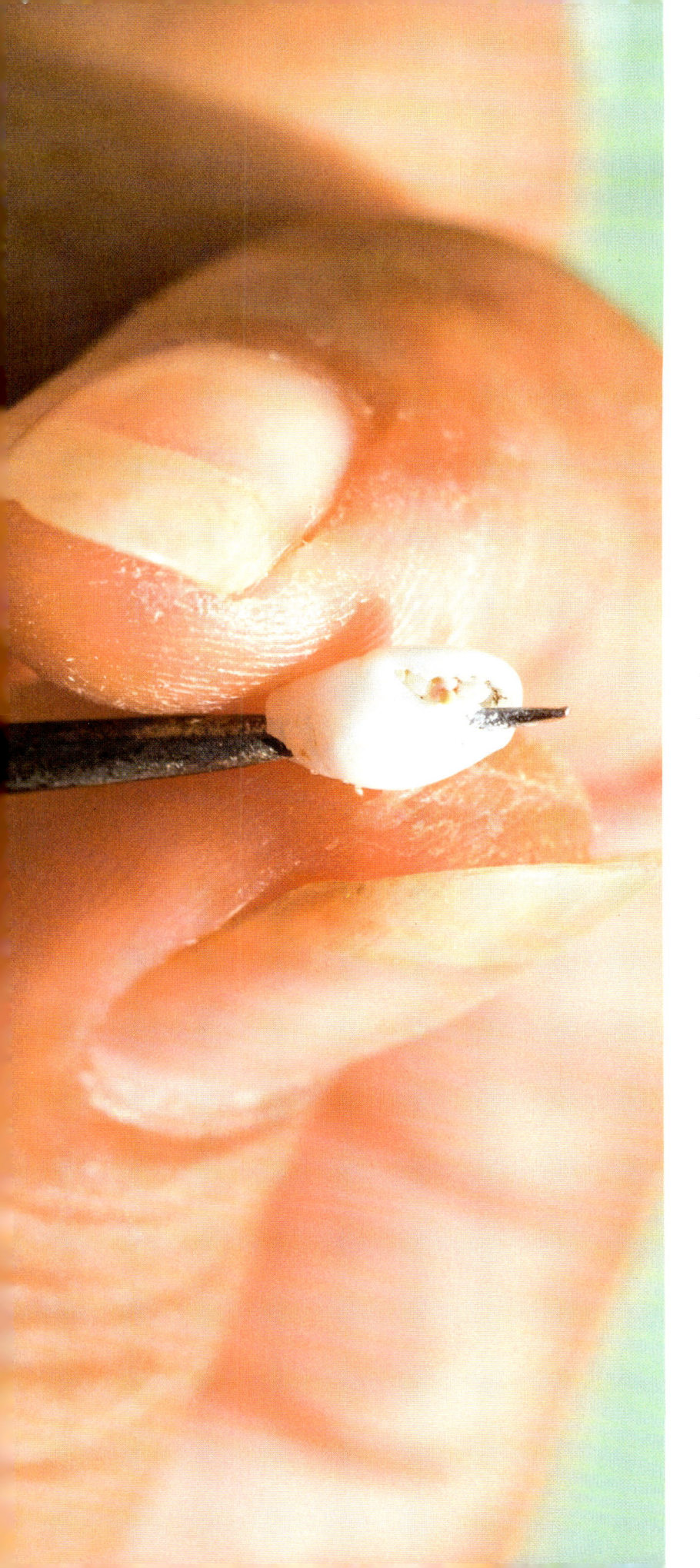

F. Cleaning the sand from the aperture.
G. Clipping the spire tip for a Lei Kui Pololei.
H. Piercing the shell.

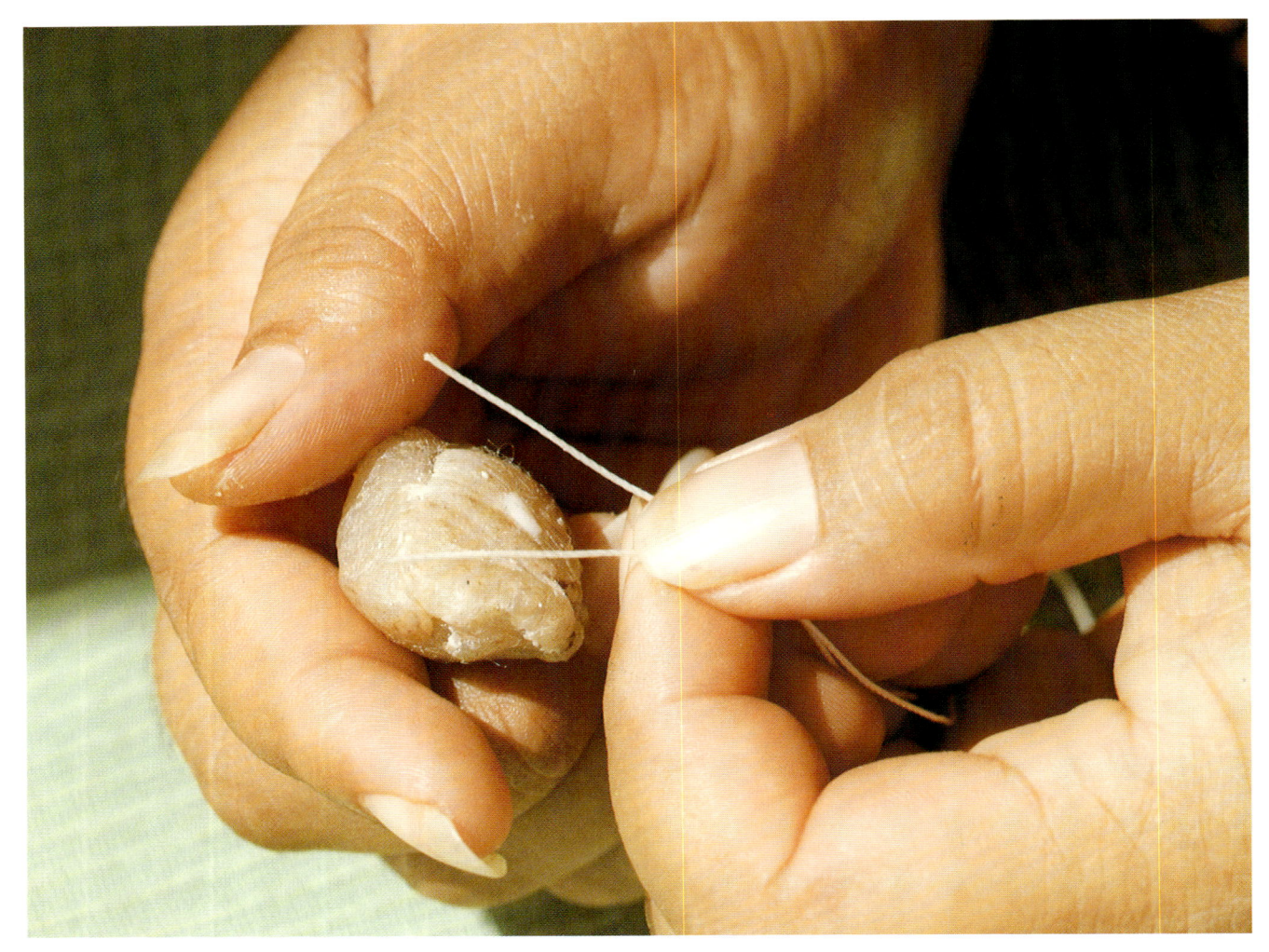

Figure I

I. Preparing the thread for stringing by passing repeatedly through beeswax.

care that is exercised by the best lei makers, an average of one out of three shells breaks during this step. Often, to make a Niʻihau shell lei 30 to 50 percent more shells are required than the ones that actually end up in the lei.

The steel awl must continually be resharpened to reduce the chances of breaking the shells and to make piercing easier. Some shells, like the laiki, have comparatively thick shells and are especially difficult to pierce.

After the shells have been pierced, a piece of nylon thread is measured and cut to the specific length of the lei to be made. One end of the thread is pushed about one inch into the top of a tube of quick-drying cement and then removed and left to dry. The resulting hardened point serves as a built-in needle for stringing.

Whatever the style, once the shells are strung to the desired length, both ends are knotted with a little thread left at each end. A kaunoʻo (sundial) or puka shell is strung onto either end. The loose ends of thread are stuffed into the aperture of the closing cowry and packed tightly into place with pieces of cotton. Some of the quick-drying

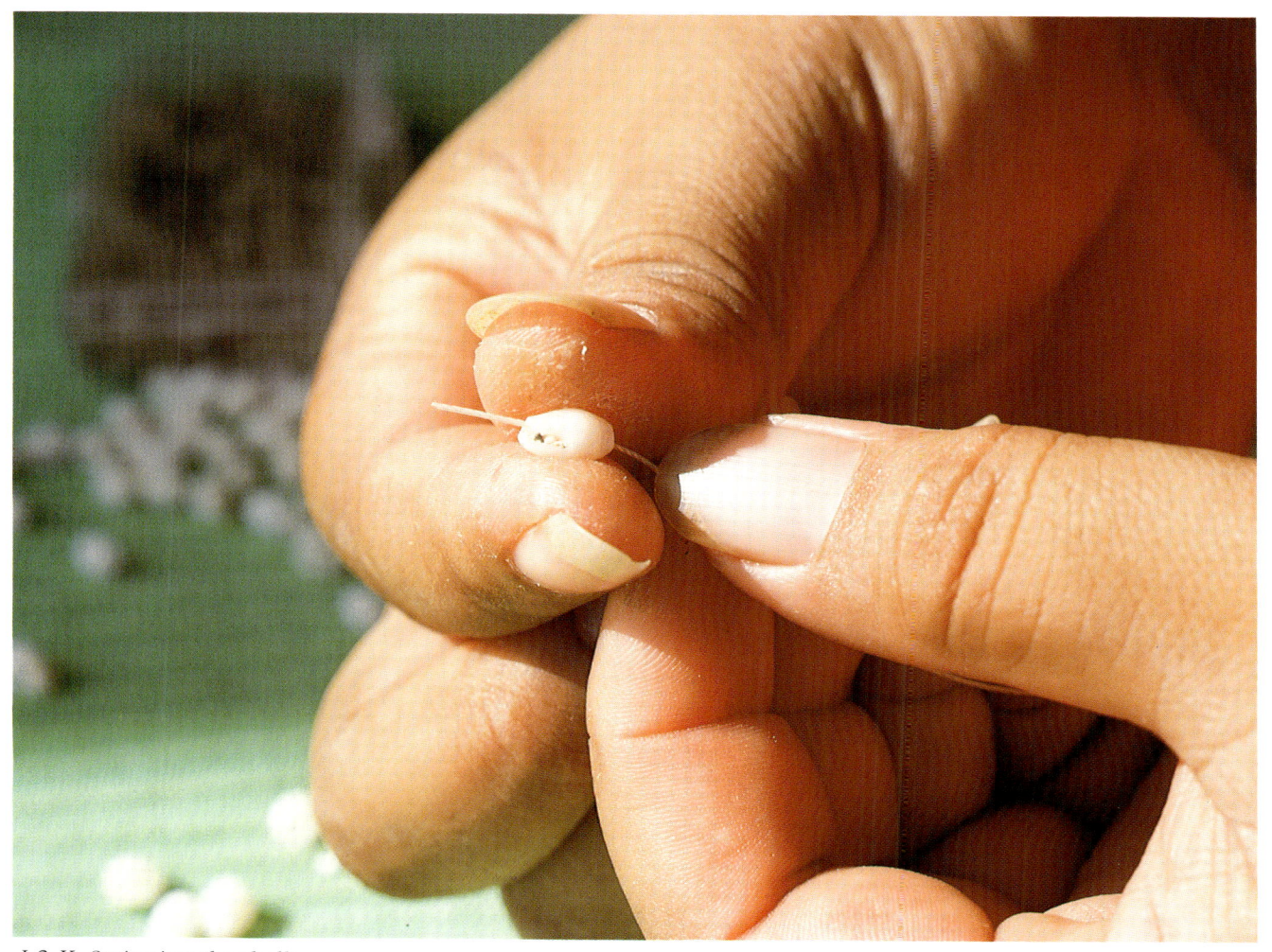

J & K. Stringing the shells.

Figure J

Figure K

L. Arranging the shells on the thread.
M. Securing the string with cotton in the aperture of the cowry.

Figure L

Figure M

N. Final closure with glue.   Figure N

cement is squeezed into the cowry's aperture, and the entire lei is set aside to allow the cement to dry. The lei is finished.

For shorter leis two cowry shells are used to join the lei, one on each end. After the thread ends and the cotton are cemented into the apertures, a hook-and-eye fastener is attached with cement to the undersides of the cowries. When the hook and the eye are fastened together, only the two cowries are visible. The fastener is concealed. Although a single or double cowry combination has always been traditionally used to join a Niʻihau shell lei, in recent years barrel clasps and other metal fasteners have been employed to join the leis, primarily for the shorter, choker-type leis.

Prior to the 1950s, before the time of quick-drying cement, many lei makers used beeswax to seal the thread ends and the cotton into the aperture of the cowry. They also ran the sewing end of the thread through the beeswax to keep it stiff enough to act as a needle. (This method is still preferred by some lei makers.) Also, instead of today's nylon thread, they used a dark green cotton thread, the same as that used for making throw nets.

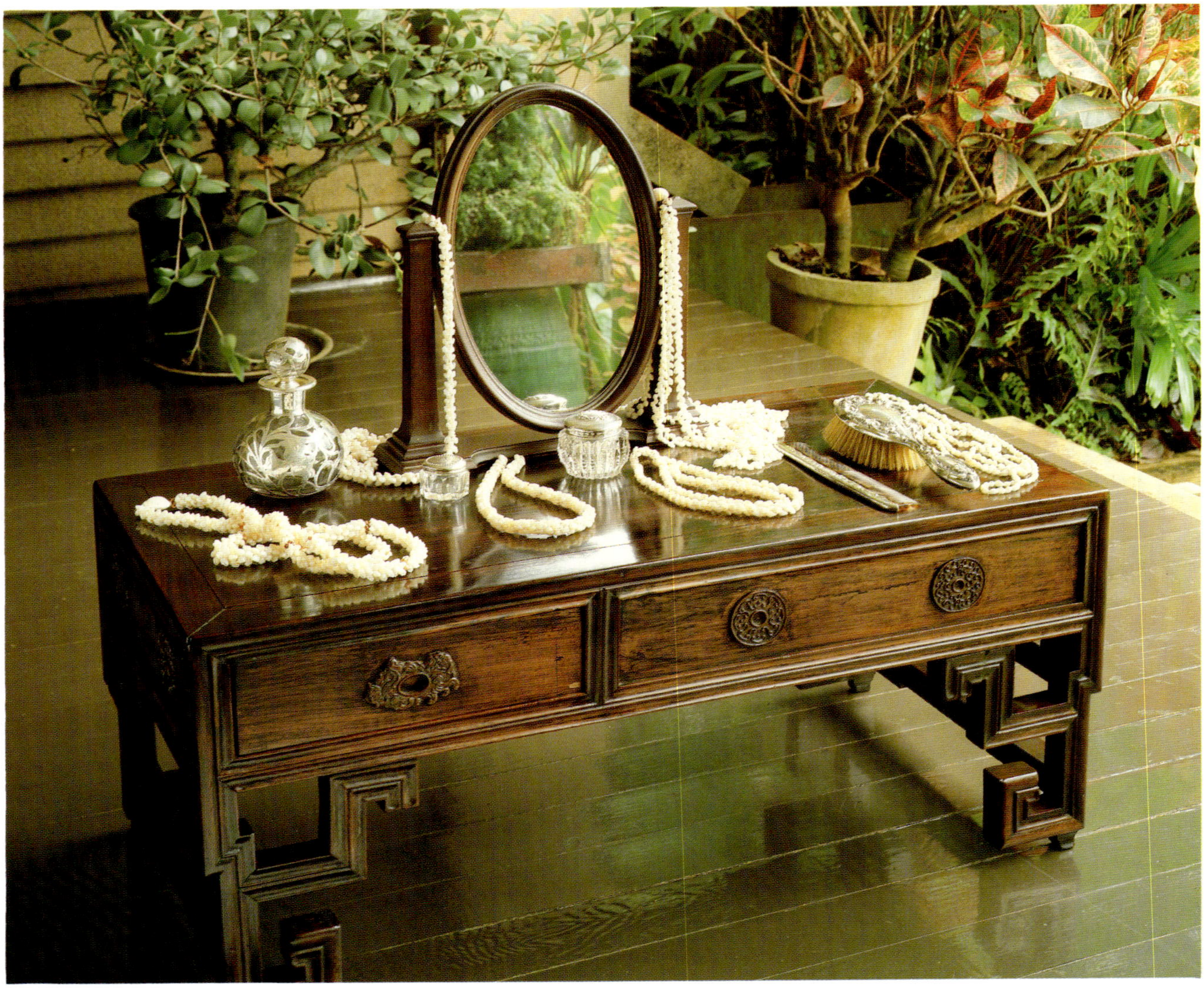

STYLES OF SEWING SHELL LEIS

Ni'ihau shell leis are named for the lei style they represent as well as for the specific shell used in the lei. For example, a singly strung Kahelelani lei could be alternately termed a Lei Kui Pololei or a Lei Kahelelani depending on whether the emphasis is on style or type of shell. Generally the lei makers favor the short version of the name, such as Lei Pikake, Lei Kipona, and Lei Kahelelani.

Lei Kui Pololei ("lei sewn straight")

This style is also known as the Single or the Old Fashioned style. The white momi or laiki shells strung in this style in lengths of 60 to 75 inches with ten to twenty strands are the traditional wedding leis of Ni'ihau. This simple sewing style was probably the original method of stringing shells for ornaments. Many of the shells that are used are found with the spire end already worn open by wave action, providing a natural hole for the lei maker. The term used for the momi and laiki shells found with the spire naturally worn open is pūpū waha nui ("shell [with a] big mouth"). Pūpū waha nui make very attractive, textured leis because the tip of one shell fits snugly into the large broken end of the next.

To prepare a momi or a laiki shell for the Lei Kui Pololei, the tip of the shell's spire, if not naturally worn off, is clipped off with a fingernail clipper. Sand grains are not removed from the aperture. The grains prevent the thread from moving out of the aperture; if this is allowed to happen, the shells turn sideways, making an uneven lei.

A collection of lei styles—a choice for the lady.
Clockwise from top left of mirror: Lei Kui Pikake (double), Lei Kui Pikake (single) also called Kui 'Ōlepelepe, Lei Kui Pololei, Lei Kui Poepoe (single), Lei Kui Poepoe (double), Lei Kui Pikake (double-double) also called Coconut.

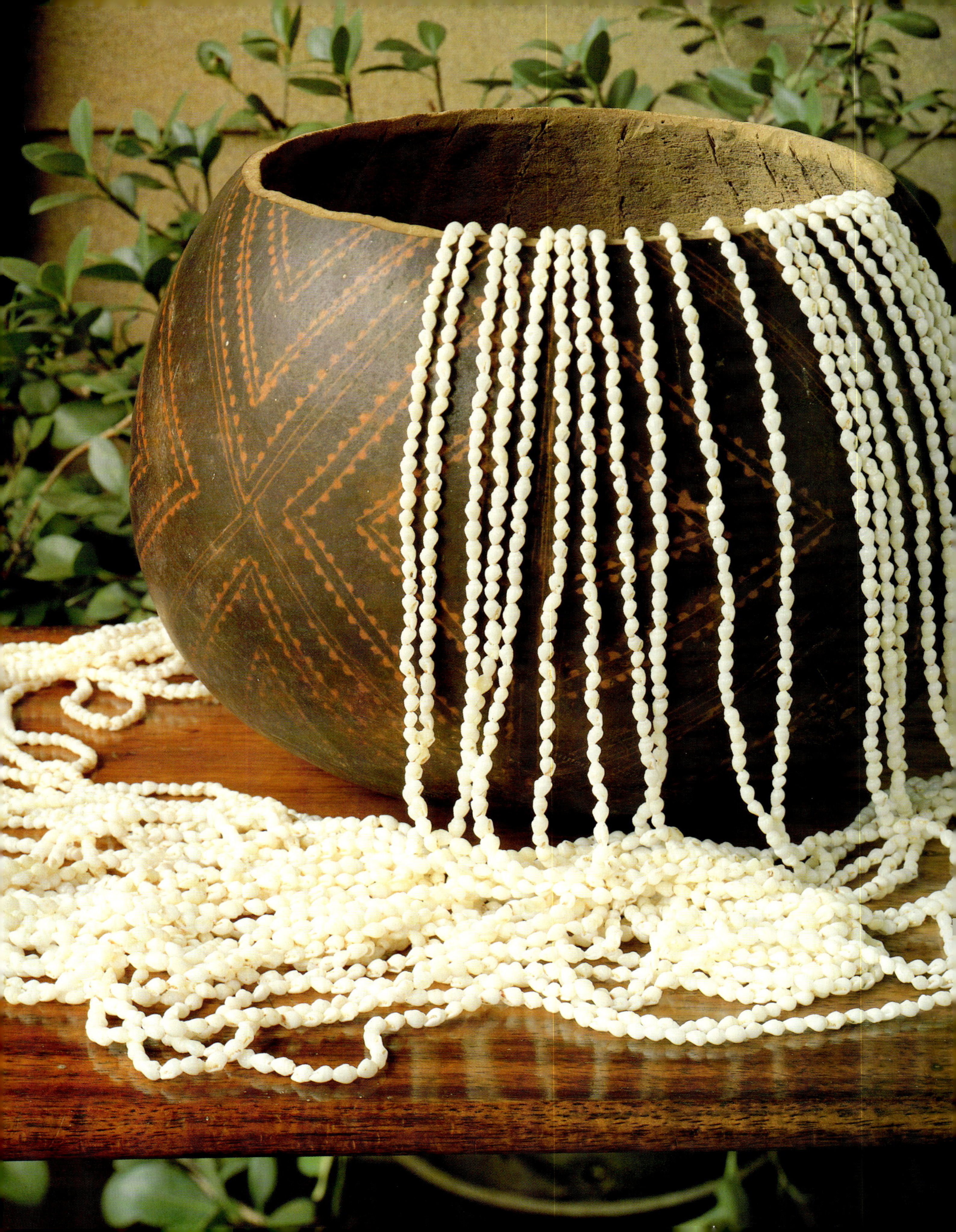

Above: *Detail of a Lei Pikake showing an interesting pattern with the consistent use of momi waha 'ele'ele or "black-mouth" tip of the momi.*

Left: *Double Pikake style with kahelelani—also called Tied Kahelelani.*

Opposite page: *Lei Kui Pololei*
Twenty strands, 60"
A classic wedding lei of momi ke'oke'o maika'i. The pure white shells cascade from a traditional decorated gourd. Ni'ihau gourd, courtesy of Grove Farm Homestead Museum; lei, courtesy of Mrs. Ruth K. Seto.

81

Once the tip is open, the awl is twisted and pushed through the spire, piercing a hole through the shell. Then the shell is strung spire end first. A single length of thread is used for each strand.

To prepare a kahelelani shell for the Lei Kui Pololei style the sand grains are cleaned out of the aperture. The awl is then inserted through the aperture, piercing a hole in the middle of the shell whorl. The shells are strung in alternating directions with the spire facing out to form a symmetrical pattern.

Lei Kui Pikake
("lei sewn [like a flower lei of] jasmine")

The people of Niʻihau call this style Pikake because the finished lei resembles a pikake or jasmine flower lei. It first appeared in the late 1940s and is now probably the most popular way to string momi shells. Although the terms Kui Pikake, or simply Pikake, commonly refer to the Double Pikake style of lei, there are actually three distinct styles of Pikake leis.

Double Pikake

A noted lei maker on Niʻihau reported that the Double Pikake style was adapted from the fancy wiliwili *(Erythrina sandwicensis)* seed leis that were popular in the Hawaiian Islands during the late 1940s. The Double Pikake style uses both momi and kahelelani shells.

To prepare the momi shells, the aperture is cleaned of sand with an awl, and then the tip of the spire is clipped off. The awl is pushed through the spire at an angle, piercing a hole in the whorl, on the side near the aperture.

Two lengths of thread are measured and each divided in half. A slipknot is made at the centers. The first shell is strung through the pierced hole and out the tip, and then another shell is strung in a like manner on the second string. The two strings are then knotted together. This pattern continues, every two shells secured with a knot, until half the lei is completed. Then the slipknot in the middle is unfastened and the other half of the lei is completed in the same manner.

When the sewing is complete, the tips of the shells face each other in the center of the lei. A skilled lei maker will often string the shells in gradually increasing size so that they are smaller at the ends and larger in the center. An interesting variation of the Double Pikake style takes advantage of the spots of the momi waha ʻulaʻula or the momi waha ʻeleʻele, allowing the spots at the bases of the shells to show in a pleasing design.

Kahelelani shells are also sewn in the Double Pikake style, but the

Above: *Lei Poepoe*
Momi kua'ula
Three strands, 36"
A fine example of a lei sewn in the Single Rope style. Courtesy of Mrs. Barbara Nishek.

Left: *Double-Double Pikake, also called Coconut style.*

83

lei makers call it the Tied Kahelelani style. To prepare the shells, a hole is made on the whorl opposite the aperture. Then the thread is pushed in, whorl-side first and out the aperture. One shell is sewn on each string of the double strings and secured by a knot. The pattern is repeated.

Single Pikake

This style is a simplified version of the Double Pikake style. The people of Niʻihau also call this style Kui ʻŌlepelepe ("sewn [by] opening and closing"). McDonald identifies it as Kui Lau.

For the Single Pikake style the momi shells are pierced as they are for the Double Pikake style, but only one length of thread is used. The shells are sewn passing the thread through the pierced hole, first with the tip of the shell facing outward, alternating side-to-side in a symmetrical pattern.

Double-Double Pikake

The people of Niʻihau also call this the Coconut style, possibly because the finished lei resembles the male inflorescense of the coconut palm. McDonald identifies it as Kui Pāhaʻa. This style uses only momi shells, pierced in the same manner as for the other Pikake styles. They are strung on four lengths of thread, one shell at a time on each of the four lengths. Two lengths of thread are held in one hand, two in the other, and a knot is made after each shell as it is placed on its respective thread. The pattern is repeated. Half of the lei is strung at a time, with the shell tips always pointing toward the center of the lei.

Lei Kui Poepoe ("lei sewn round")

This style is also called the Rope style because the finished lei resembles a rope. Usually momi shells, prepared in the same way as for the Pikake styles, are used, strung on two lengths of thread. The only difference in preparation of the shell is the position of the hole on the whorl. The hole is pierced in the middle of the whorl opposite the aperture. The position of the second hole enables the tip of the shell, when strung, to point inward and give the lei a rounded, ropelike appearance.

A recent variation of this style is called the Double Rope style. It is similar to the Double-Double Pikake style. The shells are prepared as for the Single Rope style just described, but four lengths of thread are used instead of two. The method of stringing is identical to that of the Double-Double Pikake.

Lei Wili
Momi kuaʻula, black-eyed Susan seeds (Abrus precatorius)
Outside lei, 26″
Inside lei, 26″
Hat or neck leis, circa 1950, sewn in the Kui Wili style. An exotic mixture of seeds and shells. Courtesy of Mrs. Ida Hayselden.

Lei Kui Wili ("lei sewn [by] twisting or winding")

This style is more commonly termed Lei Wili or the Wili lei. Although this style has used momi, kahelelani, and laiki shells in the past, the Lei Wili sewn on Niʻihau today uses only kahelelani shells. This style involves winding strings of shells around a cotton cloth foundation.

The kahelelani shells are prepared by first cleaning the sand grains from the aperture. Then a hole is pierced from the aperture near the siphon canal to the back whorl of the shell. The shells are strung singly, all facing the same way. After stringing 12 inches of shells, the completed section is wound around a piece of cloth that has been rolled and sewn tightly. The firm, rounded cloth foundation resembles a piece of rope, with a diameter of half an inch to one inch depending on the thickness desired for the finished lei.

When the strings of shells are wound around the cloth foundation, care is taken that the kahelelani whorls face outward. This gives a smooth, textured appearance to the lei. When the shells are even and securely in place another 12 inches of shells are strung and wound around the cloth. Starting at one end of the cloth foundation, leaving an inch or so free for joining, the finished rows of shells are closely fitted together to completely hide the cloth underneath. The leftover thread is wrapped around the cloth and knotted. Sometimes a piece of ribbon is sewn on both ends of the lei, which allows the finished lei to be tied around the neck. Another method of ending the lei is to use a kaunoʻo or puka shell and two cowries with a hook and eye closure.

Many attractive designs are found in the Wili leis. Some feature stripes, while others display more geometric patterns, such as diamonds and chevrons. The designs are created by stringing the differently colored kahelelani in repetitive progressions.

The shell leis made in the Lei Kui Wili style are usually chokers that vary in length from 18 to 22 inches. These leis are not very flexible and do not lie flat against the chest, so they are rarely made in lengths longer than neck circumference. Sometimes Wili leis are used as hat bands.

Another interesting variation of the Lei Kui Wili style appears in some of the leis from the 1930s and 1940s in which two individual shell leis, each with a different type and color of shell, were intertwined and joined with a cowry.

Lei Kui Papa ("lei sewn [in] layers")

This style was an adaptation of the Hawaiian feather lei hat bands in which the people of Niʻihau substituted ʻōlepe shells for feathers. Today these leis are very rare, and the few that still exist were strung during the 1940s and early 1950s. Kahelelani and ʻōlepe were used for

Lei Wili
Kahelelani
Top: Lei Wili with hook-and-eye closure, 22"
Middle: Lei Wili, 19"
Bottom: Lei Wili with ribbon, 19½"
Imaginative use of the varied colors of kahelelani creates interesting patterns in the lei. Courtesy of Mrs. Ruth K. Seto, Mrs. Ida Hayselden.

ALEXANDER YOUNG HOTEL
HONOLULU T. H.

Lei Kipona
Three strands, 50"
A dazzling mixture of momi kahakaha and kahelelani. Courtesy of Mrs. Ruth K. Seto.

Opposite page: *Lei Kui Papa*
A classic hat lei, circa 1930, of kahelelani made in the Kui Papa style. The lei adorns a lauhala hat beside an antique hat box, also of lauhala. Lei and hat box, courtesy of Grove Farm Homestead Museum.

Lei Kipona
Two strands and three strands, 36"
A classic interpretation of the Kipona style. These examples of Lei Kipona combine several varieties of momi sewn Pikake style and interspersed with kahelelani.
Courtesy of Mrs. Ruth K. Seto.

Opposite page: *Lei Kipona*
Momi keʻokeʻo, kahelelani ʻākala pua
Three strands, 36"
Courtesy of Mrs. Ruth K. Seto.

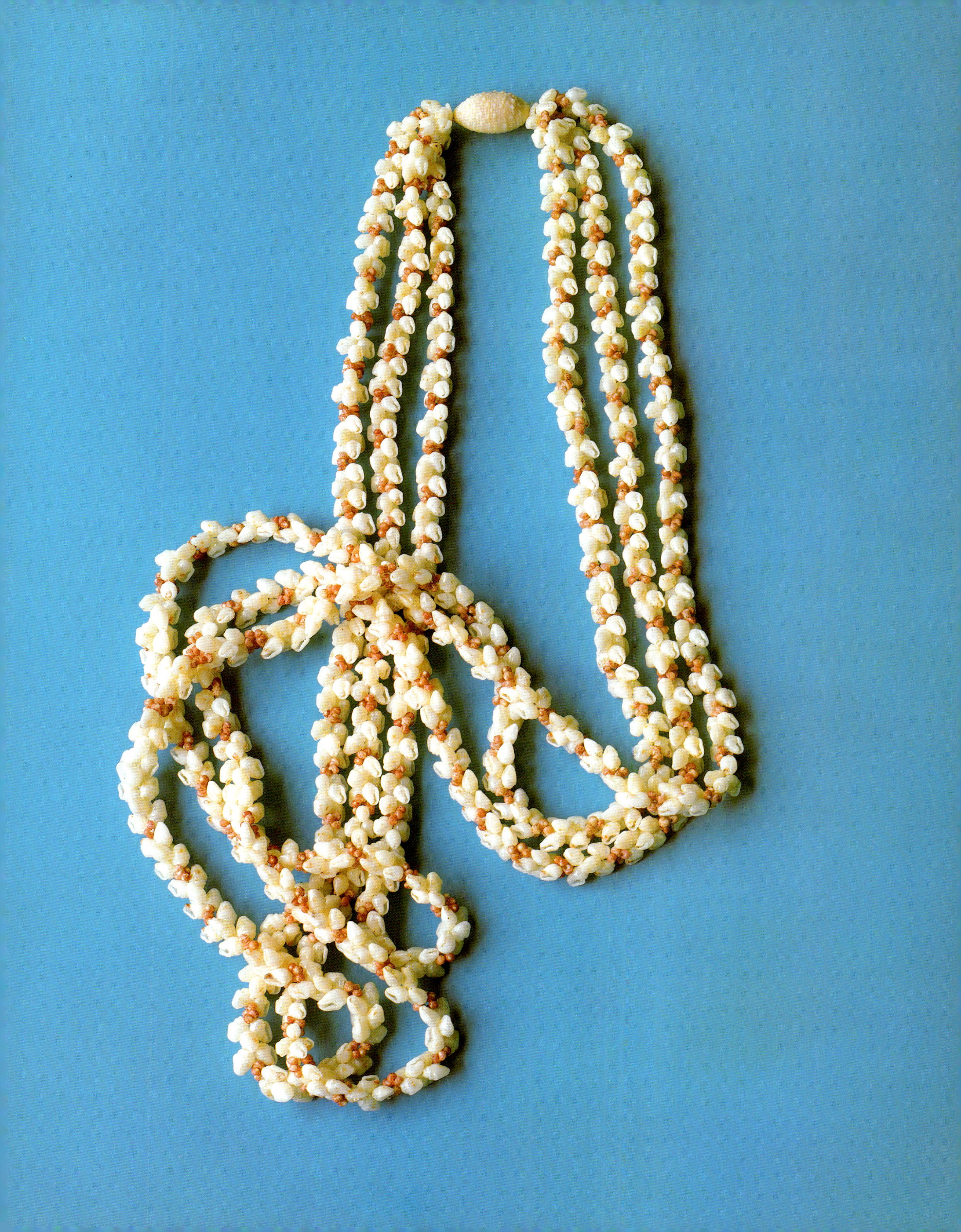

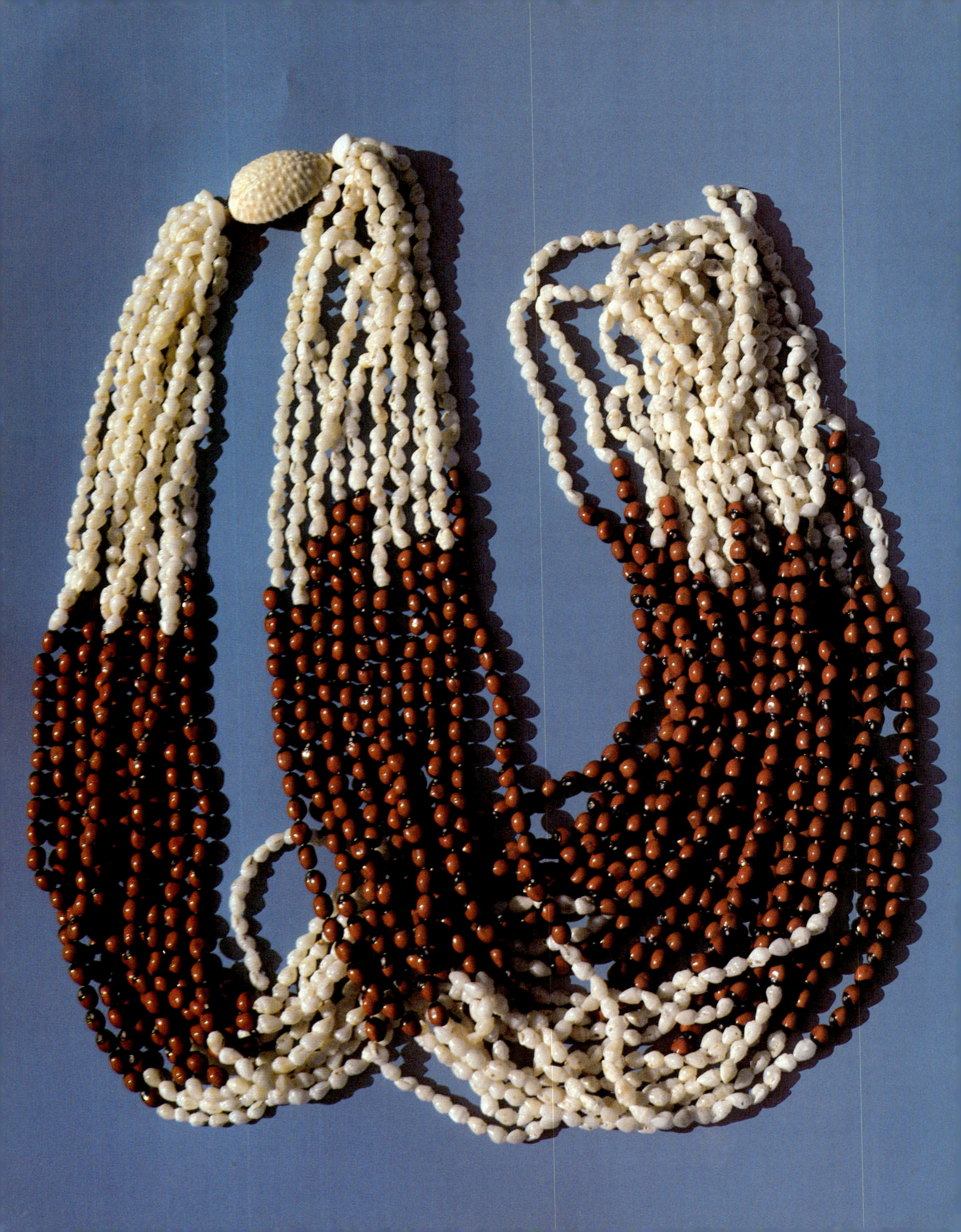

Some unusual combinations of shells and seeds.

93

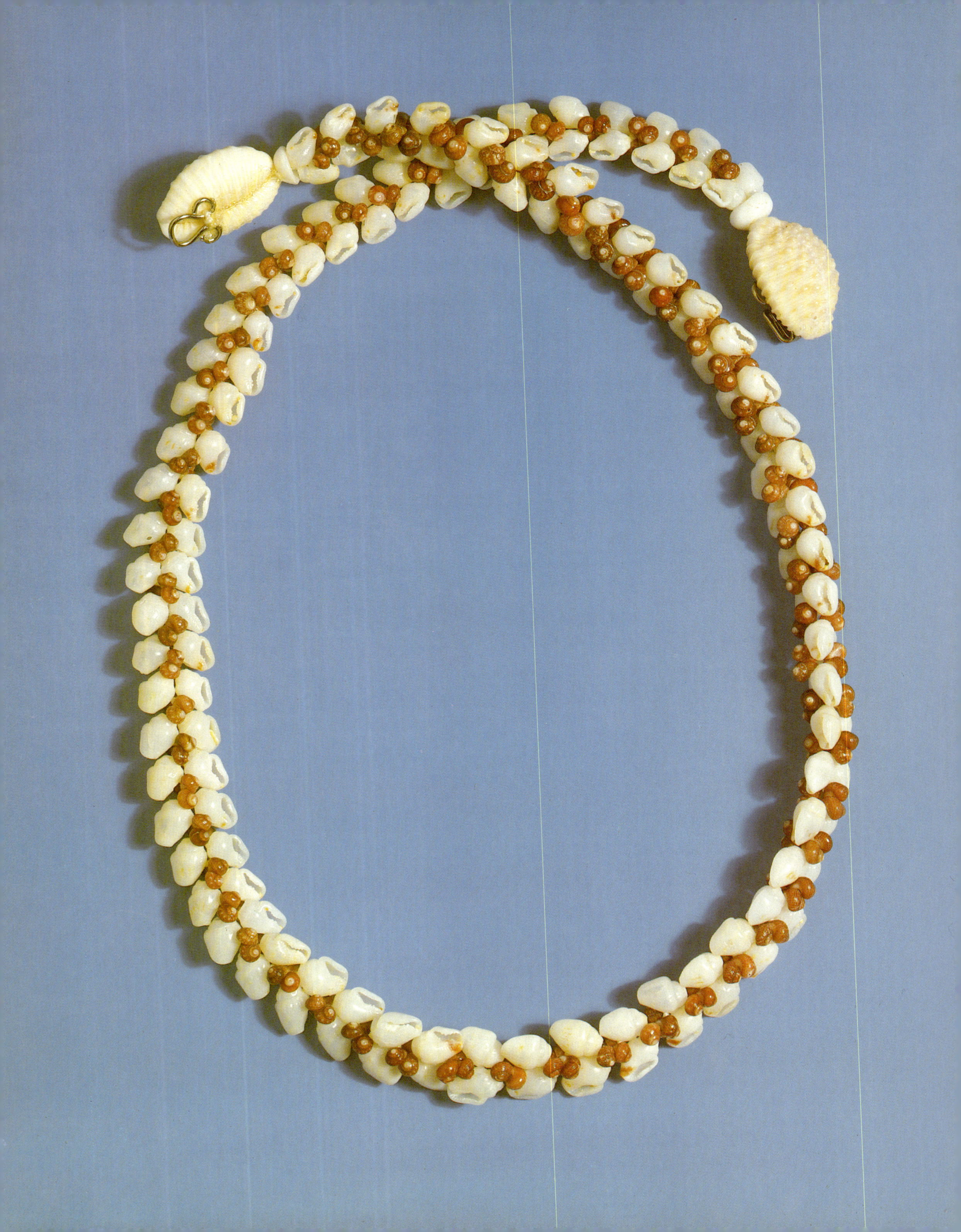

making the Lei Kui Papa. According to the older Niʻihau lei makers, only two or three women made ʻōlepe leis during that period, and in the ensuing years as the fashion of wearing hats waned, so did these lei makers' interest in sewing hat band shell leis.

Lei Kui Kipona
("lei sewn [with a] mixture [of shells]")

Any Niʻihau shell lei that displays a wide variety of shell types and color is called a Lei Kui Kipona or simply a Lei Kipona. Most Lei Kipona combine a mixture of momi and kahelelani. The lei styles vary with the types of shells used in the leis, but one common combination is momi shells sewn Pikake style with kahelelani interspersed. Other variations of the Kipona style include combinations of ʻopihi shells, puka shells, and seeds from land plants.

Lei Kui Helekonia
("lei [sewn in the likeness of a] heleconia flower")

This style is a very recent adaptation incorporating momi and kahelelani shells as in the Lei Kipona. However, a Lei Helekonia is sewn flat like the Single Pikake style, yet utilizing the two threads as in the Double Pikake style. The momi and kahelelani shells are pierced in the same manner as for the Pikake and Tied Kahelelani styles. Then they are strung using two lengths of thread. First, two momi shells are strung on each thread then knotted in place, followed by two kahelelani which are similarly strung and knotted. The pattern is repeated. Half the lei is strung at a time, with the shell tips pointing toward the center of the lei.

Lei Kui Helekonia
18"
A recently developed lei so named because it resembles the bracts and flowers of the heliconia (Heliconia sp.). *Author's collection.*

SELECTING A LEI

Niʻihau shell leis are exquisite pieces of jewelry that have been fashioned from tiny natural objects of great beauty. Some buyers select their leis solely on the basis of color, style, and length to suit their personal tastes and to complement their wardrobes, but other buyers shop for leis as they would for fine jewelry. As with any piece of fine jewelry, there are certain qualities that can be evaluated to determine the worth or excellence of a lei. In order to compare various leis and determine their quality, the following five points should be considered.

1. **Color.** The shells in a good lei have been carefully selected for color. If a lei is designed to be monochromatic, then the shells should be as nearly perfectly matched as possible. For example, if a lei is to be deemed pure white, shells that are speckled or off-white, and thus detract from the purity of the color, should not be present. In a Lei Kipona, or mixed-style lei, the selection and arrangement of shell colors should create a pleasing visual combination.

2. **Luster.** The natural luster of the shells is a very important feature to consider in selecting a lei. Shells with a brilliant luster like that of pearls are much more attractive. Shells collected on Niʻihau are generally far more radiant than those found elsewhere. The same types of shells found on Kauaʻi, for example, are inferior in color and have little or no luster. The difference is readily apparent when the two are placed side by side.

3. **Flaws.** The individual shells used in a lei should be flawless, completely free of any holes, chips, or cracks. The only holes should be the ones pierced by the lei maker. The aperture of each shell should be free of sand except in the Lei Kui Pololei style, in which the grains of sand prevent the shells from twisting on the thread and upsetting the uniformity of the style.

4. **Size.** Shells should be uniform in size, an important feature that helps determine the symmetry of the lei. If the lei is made from shells of graduated sizes, careful selection of sizes should be evident. Leis made of very tiny shells are extremely difficult to make and highly prized; the smaller the shell, the more difficult it is to clean and pierce it successfully.

5. **Workmanship.** The quality of workmanship is reflected in the piercing, sewing of the shells, and joining of the strands. The holes should be pierced in exactly the same place in each shell. This ensures evenness of style. In the Lei Kui Pololei, or single stringing style, the sewing thread should never be visible between the shells. When the sewing style requires the use of more than one length of thread, as in the Pikake styles, the knots should be tight and secure to prevent the shells from turning on the thread and upsetting the pattern.

The cowries used to join the shell leis should be of good quality, without any flaws such as chips or cracks, and the color should complement the color or colors of the lei. The loose thread and cotton stuffing should be firmly implanted and neatly glued into the aperture of the cowry. If a hook-and-eye fastener is used, it should be glued to the underside of the cowries and should not be visible to a viewer when the shells are fastened together. The kauno'o or puka shells that adjoin the cowries should match each other in size and color.

CARE AND STORAGE OF NI'IHAU SHELL LEIS

Ni'ihau shells are not as fragile as they appear; they were tossed in the high winter surf and deposited on the sand before they were collected and strung into a lei. Nonetheless, the leis do require some care.

The shells are composed of calcium carbonate and are relatively sensitive to chemicals. They absorb oils and dirt, so when a lei is worn against the skin, it should never come in contact with make-up or other chemical applications on the part of the body where the lei rests. Repeated contact with such materials will cause the shells eventually to lose their luster. Their luster may also be lost if dust is allowed to collect from constant wear or continuous open display. Ni'ihau shell leis should not be washed unless the shells are so soiled that they become discolored. At this point, they may be gently washed in a mild soap-and-water solution and set out to dry. Do not wash them, however, immediately before wearing them, for the hollow shells collect water and at least a day is needed to allow time to drain and dry out.

To properly clean a Ni'ihau shell lei, it is recommended that it be gently wiped after use with a very soft, absorbent cloth (cotton flannel) to remove any body oils and foreign chemicals. The shells should never come in contact with chlorine bleach (to whiten them), nor should they be steamed or put into any commercial jewelry cleaner.

Probably the greatest fear among Niʻihau shell lei owners and wearers is that the lei will catch or snag on something and break, reducing in seconds a painstakingly made work of art to a jar of tiny shells. This disturbing occurrence happens quite frequently with the longer leis, but fortunately the shells can be easily restrung.

For proper storage the leis should be individually wrapped in cloth or tissue paper, not in a plastic bag, and placed in a strong container with a secure lid. Finally, the container should be stored in a safe, secure place.

APPENDIX A
SCIENTIFIC DESCRIPTIONS OF NIʻIHAU SHELLS
BY E. ALISON KAY

The following account provides brief scientific descriptions of the shells used in Niʻihau shell leis.

Family Turbinidae

The Turbinidae, or turban shells, comprise a large family of globose, few-whorled shells which range in height from about 50 mm to less than 1 mm. The most famous of the turban shells are easily recognized because of the operculum, the colorful "cat's eye" of the jeweler, a thick, calcareous structure that fills the aperture of the shell. All members of the family have this characteristic solid operculum, with a heavy brown peristracum internally, often sculptured and colored externally. Turbans are herbivores and feed on algae; many are found in shallow waters of the littoral zone in the tropics and subtropics.

1. *Leptothyra verruca* (Gould, 1845). This turban shell, about 5 mm in diameter and 5 mm in height, is faintly spirally sculptured and variously colored brown, green, or red. It may be white, spirally banded with red and brown tessellations, or almost entirely brown or red. The operculum is thick and white.

These turbans are abundant on and under rocks and rubble in tide pools and on solution benches and fringing reefs. *L. verruca* was described from the Hawaiian Islands, but it occurs elsewhere in the Indo-Pacific from western Australia to the Marshall Islands.

2. *Turbo sandwicensis* (Pease, 1861). This is the largest of the Hawaiian turban shells sometimes reaching a length of more than 50 mm. The shell is solid, with a spiral sculpture of granules or scales. The shells are green or gray flashed with darker green, black, and/or brown. The thick operculum is granular, colored externally green and brown.

The Hawaiian turban is common under rocks in shallow waters shoreward of fringing reefs and on the outer edges of reefs. *T. sandwicensis* was described from the Hawaiian Islands and seems to differ in several features, such as the color and sculpture of the operculum, from another species, *T. argyrostomus* (Linnaeus, 1758), which occurs throughout the Indo-west Pacific.

Family Strombidae

The shells of the Strombidae are recognized by the outer lip, which is thick and undulated in *Strombus,* and flared and spined in *Lambis* and *Tibia.* At the anterior end there is a reflected notch, the "stromboid" notch, through which one eye of the animal protrudes. Strombids also have a unique method of locomotion: the foot is narrow and muscular and digs into the substrate enabling the animal to move by "leaping," sometimes more than a meter in distance. Strombids are herbivores, feeding on filamentous algae.

1. *Strombus maculatus* (Sowerby, 1842). The shell of *Strombus maculatus,* about 14 mm in length, is elongate, with swollen shoulders, and cream colored with brown maculations and a white aperture. A fine, transparent, yellow periostracum covers the shell.

These animals are found on intertidal solution benches and in rubble along the shore line at depths of about 2 m. *S. maculatus* occurs throughout the Pacific from Micronesia and eastern Polynesia to Easter Island but is abundant only in the Hawaiian Islands.

Family Cypraeidae

The family Cypraeidae, familiarly known as the cowries, is among the best known of all mollusks because of the highly polished, elaborately patterned shell. Cowries are found from shallow waters of the intertidal region to depths of about 100 m, and they feed on a variety of foods, some on algae, others on sponges.

1. *Cypraea annulus* (Linnaeus, 1758). These cowries, 15 to 20 mm in length, are ovate, smooth, cream colored with an orange thread around the dorsum. They do not live in Hawaiian waters, but occur throughout the Indo-west Pacific from east Africa to the Marshall Islands and the Society Islands. In the Pacific they are abundant on reefs.

2. *Cypraea caputserpentis* (Linnaeus, 1758). The snakehead cowry, about 30 mm long, is distinguished by its reticulated brown and white dorsum and brown sides. *C. caputserpentis* is the most abundant of the cowries in Hawaii, found in shallow water on reefs under loose rocks and boulders and on solution benches. The snakehead cowry occurs throughout the Indo-west Pacific, from the east coast of Africa to Clipperton Island.

3. *Cypraea granulata* (Pease, 1863). These cowries, about 25 mm in length, are easily distinguished by their granulated surface. The shells are rose-brown when live-collected but fade to creamy brown with time. The granulated surface is comprised of minute nodules joined by intervening ridges. The cowries occur at moderate depths of 3 to 15 m. *C. granulata* is endemic to the Hawaiian Islands.

4. *Cypraea helvola* (Linnaeus, 1758). This cowry, about 22 mm in length, is distinguished by its spotted and blotched purple-red to gray-brown dorsum. The extremities are pale lilac to deep purple, and the sides and base are orange-brown. The animals, common in shallow water, are probably the most common of the Hawaiian cowries at depths of about 20 m. *C. helvola* is

APPENDIX A (continued)

widely distributed in the Indo-west Pacific from the east coast of Africa to Clipperton Island off the coast of South America.

5. *Cypraea isabella* (Linnaeus, 1758). These cowries, about 32 mm in length, are cylindrical in shape, orange-brown with linear black streaks, and with the extremities dark brown. The animals are common in shallow water and have been recorded to depths of about 80 m. *C. isabella* occurs throughout the Indo-west Pacific from the east coast of Africa to Hawaii.

6. *Cypraea moneta* (Linnaeus, 1758). The money cowry, about 26 mm in length in the Hawaiian Islands, is easily recognized by its pyriform to triangular shape and pale yellow color. The sides are angular, often thickened, and sometimes nodular. Shells are uncommon in Hawaiian waters but are occasionally collected under loose rock in sand or in tide pools. Elsewhere in the Indo-west Pacific, the money cowry is abundant from East Africa to the Marshall Islands and Tahiti and has also been recorded from Clipperton Island.

7. *Cypraea sulcidentata* (Gray, 1824). This cowry, about 35 mm in length, is oval and inflated, and creamy brown in color, banded by four darker bands. The animals are found in moderately deep water, usually in coral heads. *C. sulcidentata* is endemic to the Hawaiian Islands.

Family Columbellidae

Columbellid shells are distinguished by their more or less fusiform shapes and polished, often brightly colored shells. They are remarkable for displaying an enormous range of individual variation both in color and sculpture. Some columbellids are apparently herbivores, others are carnivores.

1. *Anachis miser* (Sowerby, 1844). The shells, about 15 mm in length, are fusiform, solid, smooth or axially ribbed, and white, axially striped with black, sometimes almost entirely black or brown.

A. miser is common in shallow water, where it is often found on the fronds of seaweeds such as *Sargassum* and *Galaxiura*. This species is found throughout the Indo-west Pacific.

2. *Euplica varians* (Sowerby, 1832). These shells, about 10 mm in length, are conical, solid, with a wide shoulder, and noduled below the suture on the last whorl. They are extremely variable in color, some white, the base stained dark blue, others splashed or lineated with black or brown.

These columbellids are abundant, found on rocks in tide pools, in shallow water shoreward of fringing reefs. *E. varians* was described from the Galapagos Islands, but the name is widely used for the species, which is found throughout the Indo-west Pacific.

3. *Mitrella margarita* (Reeve, 1859). These shells, 10 mm in length, are ovate, smooth, and shining. They are ivory, stained with yellow-brown lineations and freckles, often with a spiral of white and brown below the suture.

These shells are often found in beach drift, but appear to live in deeper water than do either *Anachis miser* or *Euplica varians*, and shells have been found in sediments to depths of 100 m.

M. margarita was described from the Hawaiian Islands, but is distributed throughout the Indo-west Pacific and occurs in Mauritius and New Caledonia.

Family Architectonicidae

Architectonicid shells are low-spired, the whorls coiled on a wide axis, and the umbilicus is often open all the way to the apex. Architectonicids feed on corals and sea anemones.

1. *Heliacus variegatus* (Gmelin, 1791). The shells, about 12 mm in diameter and 9 mm in length, are turbiniform, with inflated, convex whorls spirally sculptured by small granules, and variegated brown and black. This is the most commonly found species of architectonicid in Hawaiian waters; it is found living with sea anemones of the genus *Palythoa*.

H. variegatus occurs throughout the Indo-west Pacific, from the Seychelles and Sri Lanka to the Marquesas Islands.

Family Melampidae

The melampids are pulmonates, found high along the shore line where they are beyond the reach of the tides, but within the reach of spray and salt air. Gregarious animals, they may be found by many hundreds in a colony.

1. *Melampus castaneus* (Muhlfeld, 1816). The shells, about 13 mm in length and 7 mm in diameter, are ovate, the last whorl the largest and the spire short, smooth, and dark brown. The shells are light to dark brown, the aperture lighter. These melampids are found in the supraspray zone under rocks and rubble. *M. castaneus* is known throughout the tropical Pacific.

Family Pectinidae

The pectens, or scallops, comprise a large group of bivalves, which are most abundant and attain their largest size in temperate waters. Pecten shells are more or less circular in outline with a straight hinge and two projections on each valve along the straight line of the hinge. The right valve is usually identified by a notch through which the bys-

APPENDIX A (continued)

sus passes. In some species the two valves of the shell are similar (equivalve); in others the two valves are quite different (inequivalve). The external surface of the valves is usually radially ridged and often tinted with bright colors.

1. *Chlamys irregularis* (Sowerby, 1842). The valves, often more than 30 mm in height and 27 mm in diameter, are subcircular, thin, barely inflated, and inequivalve. They are white to yellow, variegated with red and brown blotches; the interior is rose or yellow, with darker spots. These pectens are uncommon, found at depths of 12 to 150 m. *C. irregularis* was described from "Eastern Seas" and may be found elsewhere in the Pacific in addition to Hawaii.

2. *Haumea juddi* (Dall, Bartsch and Rehder, 1938). In these pectens the valves, 19 mm in height and 18 mm in length, are subcircular, moderately solid, and distinctly inequivalve. The right valve is white with a reddish spot at the umbo; the left valve is mottled and banded with red brown. They are common to abundant at depths of from 8 to 100 m. *H. juddi* was described from the Hawaiian Islands.

APPENDIX B
NI'IHAU SHELL LEIS IN MUSEUM COLLECTIONS

Bernice P. Bishop Museum
P.O. Box 19000-A
Honolulu, HI 96817

HH 111, HH 272, HH 273, HH 274, HH 278, HH 464 (640), HH 465 (641), HH 645, HH 646, HH 647, HH 648, HH 1109, HH 1514, 270.03, 1345, 6770

Daughters of Hawaii
Hulihe'e Place
P.O. Box 1838
Kailua-Kona, HI 96745

1571

Field Museum of Natural History
Roosevelt Road at Lake Shore Drive
Chicago, IL 60605

272604

Kauai Museum
Lihue, HI 96766

1985.271, 1985.272, 1985.273, 1985.274, 1985.275

Lyman House Museum
276 Haili Street
Hilo, HI 96720

85.7.3, 00.1512, 00.1658, 00.1661

Museum of Archaeology and
    Anthropology
University of Cambridge
Downing Street
Cambridge CB2 3DZ, U.K.

27.1638, 27.1639

Museum of Mankind
Ethnology Department of the
    British Museum
Burlington Gardens
London W1X 2EX, U.K.

HAW 122, Q77 Oc.4, Q80 Oc.961, Q80 Oc.962, Q80 Oc.963, Q80.964, Q80 Oc.965, Q80 Oc.977, Q80 Oc.978, VAN 277 a and b, VAN 278

Peabody Museum
Harvard University
11 Divinity Avenue
Cambridge, MA 02138

D-2934, 37.646, 86-14(47746)

Peabody Museum of Salem
East India Square
Salem, MA 01976

E 16.783, E 16.872, E 16.874, E 21.510, E 34.695, E 35.455

BIBLIOGRAPHY

Beaglehole, John C., ed. *The Journals of Captain James Cook on His Voyages of Discovery . . .* 3 vols. Cambridge: At the University Press (published for the Hakluyt Society), 1955–1967.

Bird, Isabella. Letters from the Sandwich Islands written to her sister between Feb. 19, 1873, and June 5, 1873. Unpublished. John Murray, Ltd. London.

Bird, Isabella. *Six Months in the Sandwich Islands.* Honolulu: University of Hawaii Press (published for the Friends of the Library of Hawaii), 1964.

Bryan, E. H. "Pikake Shells." *Paradise of the Pacific,* vol. 53, no. 4. April 1941.

Bryan, William Alanson. *Natural History of Hawaii.* Honolulu: The Hawaii Gazette Co., 1915.

Buck, Peter H. *Arts and Crafts of Hawaii.* Section 12. Bernice P. Bishop Museum Special Publication 45. Honolulu: Bishop Museum Press, 1957.

Cook, James, et al. *A Voyage to the Pacific Ocean . . . for Making Discoveries in the Northern Hemisphere . . . in the Years 1776, 1777, 1778, 1779, and 1780.* 3 vols. London: W. and A. Strahan, 1784.

Cross, E. R. "Shell Collector's Notebook." *Skin Diver Magazine,* April 1978.

Daws, Gavan, and Timothy Head. "Niihau: A Shoal of Time." *American Heritage,* vol. 14, no. 6. October 1963.

Dixon, G. *A Voyage Around the World . . . 1785–88.* London: G. Goulding, 1789.

Emma, Queen. Letter to Sarah Weed, March 20, 1871. Bernice P. Bishop Museum, Henriques Collection.

Edmondson, Charles Howard. *Reef and Shore Fauna of Hawaii.* Bernice P. Bishop Museum Special Publication 22. Honolulu: Bishop Museum Press, 1946.

Finney, B. L. *Directory and Reference Book of the Hawaiian Islands 1896–7.* Honolulu: Published by B. L. Finney, 1897.

Forbes, David. *Queen Emma and Lawai.* Kauai: Kauai Historical Society, April 1970.

Gay, Lawrence K. *Tales of the Forbidden Island of Niʻihau.* Honolulu: Topgallant Publishing Co., 1981.

Gilman, La Selle. "Invasion by Haoles at Niʻihau." *Paradise of the Pacific,* vol. 55, no. 12. December 1943.

Grant, M. Forsyth. *Scenes in Hawaii or Life in the Sandwich Islands.* Toronto: Hart & Co., 1888.

Ho, Ramona. Niʻihau, a Bibliography. Typescript, Hamilton Library, University of Hawaii, 1978.

Jarves, James Jackson. *History of the Hawaiian or Sandwich Islands.* London: Tappan and Dennet, 1843.

Jernigan, E. W. "The Cloud in the Shell." *Arizona Highways.* October 1981.

Judd, Henry P. "A Week on Niʻihau." *Paradise of the Pacific,* vol. 50, no. 9. September 1938.

Kaeppler, Adrienne L. *Artificial Curiosities.* Bernice P. Bishop Museum Special Publication 65. Honolulu: Bishop Museum Press, 1978.

Kanahele, George S. *Hawaiian Music and Musicians: An Illustrated History.* Honolulu: University Press of Hawaii, 1979.

Kay, E. Alison. *Hawaiian Marine Shells.* Bernice P. Bishop Museum Special Publication 64(4). Honolulu: Bishop Museum Press, 1979.

Malinowski, Bronislaw. *Argonauts of the Western Pacific.* London: G. Routledge & Sons, 1922.

McCool, Makana, Penny Nitta, and Donna Yadao. "Niihau Shell Lei Making." *Moʻolelo,* vol. 1, no. 2. Kauai High School, March 1976.

McDonald, Marie A. *Ka Lei.* Honolulu: Topgallant Publishing Co., 1978.

"OPA-Hawaiian Style." *Paradise of the Pacific,* vol. 55, no. 5. May 1943.

Pukui, Mary Kawena. *ʻŌlelo Noʻeau, Hawaiian Proverbs and Poetical Sayings.* Bernice P. Bishop Museum Special Publication 71. Honolulu: Bishop Museum Press, 1983.

Pukui, Mary Kawena, and Samuel H. Elbert. *Hawaiian Dictionary.* Honolulu: University of Hawaii Press, 1971.

Pukui, Mary Kawena, Samuel H. Elbert, and Esther T. Mookini. *Place Names of Hawaii.* Honolulu: The University Press of Hawaii, 1974.

Pukui, Mary, and Marie Neal. "The Leis of Hawaii." *Paradise of the Pacific,* vol. 55, no. 12. December 1941.

Quiggin, A. Hingston. *A Survey of Primitive Money.* New York: Barnes & Noble, 1970.

Safer, Jane Fearer, and Frances McLaughlin Gill. *Spirals from the Sea.* New York: Clarkson N. Potter, 1982.

Samwell, David. Some Account of a Voyage to the South Seas (:) in 1776–1777–1778. Unpublished manuscript (author's journal covering the period February 10, 1977–November 29, 1779). Original copy in the British Museum.

Schmitt, Robert C. "Unchanged Niihau." *Paradise of the Pacific,* vol. 66, no. 5. May 1954.

Shideler, Harpe. "Niihau, the Forbidden Island." *Paradise of the Pacific,* vol. 73, no. 4. April 1961.

Soehren, Lloyd. Archaeology at Nualolo-kai. Unpublished manuscript, Department of Anthropology, Bernice P. Bishop Museum, Honolulu, ca. 1960.

Titcomb, Margaret, et al. "Native Use of Marine Invertebrates in Old Hawaii." *Pacific Science,* vol. 32, no. 4 (1978). Honolulu: The University Press of Hawaii, 1979.

Thrum, Thomas G. *Hawaiian Annual for 1922.* Honolulu: Thomas G. Thrum, 1921.

Vancouver, George. *A Voyage of Discovery to the North Pacific Ocean and Round the World. . . .* New York: DaCapo Press, 1967.

Webb, Elizabeth Lahilahi Rogers. "The Pupu Niihau or Niihau Shell." *Paradise of the Pacific,* vol. 52, no. 8. August 1940.